Best Easy Day Hikes
Phoenix

Help Us Keep This Guide Up to Date

Every effort has been made by the author and editors to make this guide as accurate and useful as possible. However, many things can change after a guide is published—trails are rerouted, regulations change, techniques evolve, facilities come under new management, etc.

We appreciate hearing from you concerning your experiences with this guide and how you feel it could be improved and kept up to date. While we may not be able to respond to all comments and suggestions, we'll take them to heart and we'll also make certain to share them with the author. Please send your comments and suggestions to the following email address:

FalconGuides
Reader Response/Editorial Department
Falconeditorial@rowman.com

Thanks for your input, and happy trails!

Best Easy Day Hikes Series

Best Easy Day Hikes Phoenix

Fourth Edition

Stewart M. Green

FALCONGUIDES

ESSEX, CONNECTICUT

FALCONGUIDES®

An imprint of The Globe Pequot Publishing Group, Inc.
64 South Main Street
Essex, CT 06426
www.globepequot.com

Distributed by NATIONAL BOOK NETWORK

British Library Cataloguing-in-Publication Information available

Library of Congress Cataloging-in-Publication Data

Names: Green, Stewart M., author.
Title: Best easy day hikes Phoenix / Stewart M. Green.
Description: Fourth edition. | Essex, Connecticut : FalconGuides, [2024] |
    Summary: "With hikes varying from half-hour strolls to full-day adventures, this guidebook has something for everyone, including families"—Provided by publisher.
Identifiers: LCCN 2024002915 (print) | LCCN 2024002916 (ebook) | ISBN 9781493075485 (paperback) | ISBN 9781493075492 (epub)
Subjects: LCSH: Hiking—Arizona—Phoenix—Guidebooks. |
    Trails—Arizona—Phoenix—Guidebooks. | Phoenix (Ariz.)—Guidebooks.
Classification: LCC GV199.42.A72 P4843 2024 (print) | LCC GV199.42.A72 (ebook) | DDC 796.5109791/73—dc23/eng/20240122
LC record available at https://lccn.loc.gov/2024002915
LC ebook record available at https://lccn.loc.gov/2024002916

Dedicated to the memory of my nephew,
Blake Harrison Green (1989–2014).
Beloved son, grandson, nephew, cousin, and friend.
We love you, Blake.
See you on the other side of the mountain.

Overview

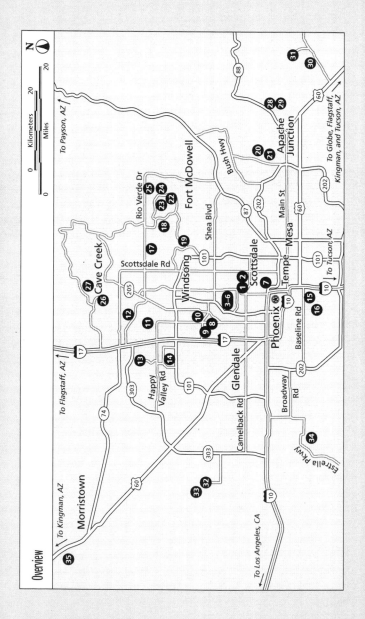

Contents

Acknowledgments

I love hiking and climbing around the Phoenix area, grabbing handholds on volcanic and granite cliffs, putting one foot in front of the other on rocky desert trails, and scrambling to the arid summits of rocky peaks with forever views. My sincere thanks to my friends, family, and park rangers who have hiked with me, met along the trail, provided info and guidance, and those knowledgeable folks at the Phoenix and Maricopa County parks who gave suggestions, reviewed chapters, and made corrections, including Patricia Armstrong, Brian Shelton, Ian Green, Aubrey Green, Rand Hubbell, Jewels Johnson, Marty Karabin, John Loleit, Martha Morris, Albert Newman, Diane Beilmann Harris, and Jim Waugh. Also, my gracious thanks to my editors, mapmaker, and sales staff at FalconGuides, the Globe Pequot Publishing Group, Inc., and National Book Network for working with me on this comprehensive new fourth edition of *Best Easy Day Hikes Phoenix*, including Mason Gadd, Max Phelps, Nicole Carty, and Melissa Baker.

Map Legend

══⟨90⟩══	Interstate Highway
══⟨30⟩══	US Highway
══⟨20⟩══	State Highway
══[41]══	Country Road
═════	Local Road
= = = = =	Unimproved Road
- - - - - - -	Trail
▬▬▬▬▬	Featured Trail
▬▬▬▬▬	Paved Trail
∿	River
–··–	Intermittent Stream
▦	State/Regional Park
▦	National Forest/Park
⌣	Bridge
■	Building/Point of Interest
▲	Campground
⌢⌢⌢	Cliff
⌶	Gate
❷	Information/Visitor Center
🅿	Parking
⌣	Pass
▲	Peak
🎪	Picnic Area
×	Point Elevation
🏠	Ranger Station
🚻	Restroom
❀	Scenic View/Overlook
❶	Trailhead

Introduction

The Phoenix metropolitan area, sprawling across the Valley of the Sun, is one of Arizona's most popular visitor destinations. The city and its suburbs, including Scottsdale, Tempe, and Glendale, offer superb hiking trails on the area's many mountains and mountain ranges. *Best Easy Day Hikes Phoenix* describes thirty-five of the best and most accessible trails for the casual hiker.

If you are on a tight schedule or want to do a short, excellent hike in a scenic area, this book allows you to quickly select a hike suited to your abilities and time constraints. Most of the hikes are between 1 and 3 miles long, round-trip. Also included are easy walks for families and barrier-free trails that are wheelchair accessible. All the trailheads are easily accessible by car and have parking lots.

The hikes are rated by difficulty from easiest to most challenging. Check the hike planning information at the beginning of each chapter to help you decide which hike is best for you and your party.

Weather

All the described hikes in the Phoenix area lie in the Sonoran Desert. The best months for hiking are October through April. Daily high temperatures can be extreme, particularly in summer when temperatures can reach 120°F. The sun can be hot even in the cooler months and shade is seldom found. Always carry adequate water to avoid dehydration and heat exhaustion. A quart per person for a 3-mile hike is not too much; more is better. It's also important to wear a hat to shade your face. Use sunscreen. Good hiking boots protect your feet from rough rocks and cactus spines. Although it's unlikely you will see a rattlesnake, keep alert for snakes on the trail or under nearby rocks.

The trails and access points are all on public land administered by the Phoenix Parks and Recreation Department, Maricopa County Parks and Recreation Office, Arizona State Parks, Tonto National Forest, and other agencies. More information on these and other area trails is available from these agencies.

Types of Hikes

Loop: A loop hike starts and ends at the same trailhead via different routes, although part of the hike may retrace the same route for a short distance.

Out and back: An out-and-back hike reaches a specific destination and returns via the same route. Distances given in the text are specified as one way (just the out portion) or round trip (out and back).

Trail Maps

Detailed maps of all the different hiking trails are included in this book. If you need more maps, many others are available for hikers. USGS topographic maps for each hike are listed, although they are out of date since many of the trails and the surrounding suburban areas and roads have changed and grown since they were first published. A color map of the Phoenix Mountains Preserve trails is available from the Phoenix Parks and Recreation Department. Hiking trail maps are available at visitor contact stations in the Maricopa County and Arizona state parklands. Maps are also available on the Internet at the various public agencies that administer the parks. Check the appendix for websites, mailing addresses, and phone numbers for the appropriate agencies.

Zero Impact

Phoenix and the surrounding mountain ranges lie in the Sonoran Desert ecosystem, an area characterized by extreme temperatures and giant cacti. Desert ecosystems and environments are extremely fragile and sensitive to human use. The marks of man linger for a long time on this arid landscape. Irrigation canals built by the ancient Hohokam Indians over a thousand years ago can still be seen. More recent scars include old mines, social trails, and damage from off-road vehicles and motorcycles.

Desert hikers should adopt a zero-impact ethic to minimize their impact on this beautiful land. The trails in the Phoenix area are heavily used and sometimes abused. As trail users and advocates, we need to pay attention to the impact that our hiking has on the landscape. If we all obey some commonsense rules for desert hiking, we can ensure that these fabulous trails will remain as a wild retreat from the encroaching city.

To minimize your impact, follow these three principles.

Three Falcon Zero-Impact Principles
Leave with everything you brought.
Leave no sign of your visit.
Leave the landscape as you found it.

Always stay on the trail. Cutting switchbacks or traveling cross-country causes erosion and destroys plants. Often a trail is braided; try to follow the main route whenever possible.

The desert is very susceptible to erosion caused by unthinking off-trail hiking.

Pack it in—pack it out. Everything you carry and use, including food wrappers, orange peels, cigarette butts, and plastic bottles, needs to come out with you. Carry a bag for picking up other trash along the trail.

Respect public and private property, livestock fences, and mining claims. Federal laws protect all archaeological and historic antiquities, including Indian ruins and artifacts, petroglyphs, fossilized bone and wood, and historic sites. Leave all natural features like flowers or rocks where you found them. Enjoy their beauty but leave them for the next hiker.

Properly dispose of human waste by digging a hole 4 to 6 inches deep and at least 300 feet from water sources and dry washes. Do not burn or bury toilet paper. Instead, pack it out in a plastic baggie. The best thing to do, of course, is to use the public restrooms that are found at most of the trailheads described in this book.

Take only photographs and memories. We can easily avoid leaving any evidence of our passage across this lovely and delicate desert environment. With a bit of care and sensitivity, we can all do our part to keep the desert beautiful, clean, and pristine. Don't pick flowers, pick up rocks, or take anything with you when you leave. If everyone took just one item, it wouldn't be long before nothing was left. Leave your souvenirs for other hikers to enjoy.

Ranking the Hikes

The hikes in this book range from easy to challenging, depending on the length of the hike as well as the elevation gain. Some hikes, like those at Camelback Mountain and Piestewa Peak, are relatively short but are also steep and strenuous with sharp grades and lots of elevation gain. Here's a list of all the hikes from easiest to most challenging.

Trail Finder

Best Hikes for Summits

2. Camelback Mountain/Echo Canyon Recreation Area: Cholla Trail
3. Piestewa Peak Recreation Area: Summit Trail
10. Lookout Mountain Park: Summit Trail
11. Phoenix Sonoran Preserve: Union Peak Loop
14. Thunderbird Conservation Park: Arrowhead Point Trail

Best Hikes for Children

4. Piestewa Peak Recreation Area: Nature Trail
7. Papago Park: Double Butte Loop Trail
15. South Mountain Park: Dirt Road Trail-Pima Wash Trail
21. Usery Mountain Regional Park: Merkle Trail
33. White Tank Mountain Regional Park: Waterfall Trail

Best Hikes for Great Views

3. Piestewa Peak Recreation Area: Summit Trail
27. Spur Cross Ranch Conservation Area: Spur Cross and Metate Trails
2. Camelback Mountain/Echo Canyon Recreation Area: Cholla Trail
20. Usery Mountain Regional Park: Wind Cave Trail
31. Superstition Wilderness Area: Peralta Trail

Best Hikes for Solitude

30. Peralta Regional Park: Saguaro Loop Trail
27. Spur Cross Ranch Conservation Area: Spur Cross and Metate Trails
11. Phoenix Sonoran Preserve: Union Peak Loop
20. Usery Mountain Regional Park: Wind Cave Trail
23. McDowell Mountain Regional Park: Wagner-Granite-Bluff Trails Loop

Best Hikes for Geology

17. Pinnacle Peak Park: Pinnacle Peak Trail
18. McDowell Sonoran Preserve: Tom's Thumb, Feldspar, and Marcus Landslide Loop
29. Lost Dutchman State Park: Siphon Draw Trail
31. Superstition Wilderness Area: Peralta Trail

Best Hikes for a Workout

1. Camelback Mountain/Echo Canyon Recreation Area: Echo Canyon Trail
3. Piestewa Peak Recreation Area: Summit Trail
8. North Mountain Park: North Mountain National Trail
9. North Mountain Park: Shaw Butte Trail

Best Hikes for Birders

11. Phoenix Sonoran Preserve: Union Peak Loop
17. Pinnacle Peak Park: Pinnacle Peak Trail
18. McDowell Sonoran Preserve: Tom's Thumb, Feldspar, and Marcus Landslide Loop
26. Cave Creek Regional Park: Go John Trail
31. Superstition Wilderness Area: Peralta Trail

Best Hikes for Cactus Gardens

27. Spur Cross Ranch Conservation Area: Spur Cross and Metate Trails
30. Peralta Regional Park: Saguaro Loop Trail
11. Phoenix Sonoran Preserve: Union Peak Loop
19. McDowell Sonoran Preserve: Horseshoe Loop Hike
12. Phoenix Sonoran Preserve: Apache Wash Trails Loop

1 Camelback Mountain/Echo Canyon Recreation Area: Echo Canyon Trail

This strenuous and popular hike, one of the most popular in Phoenix, climbs past cliffs and cactus to the rocky summit of 2,704-foot-high Camelback Mountain.

Distance: 2.4 miles
Hiking time: 1–3 hours
Type of hike: Out and back
Trail name: Echo Canyon Trail
Difficulty: Strenuous due to steepness and technical terrain. Cumulative elevation gain is 1,414 feet.
Best season: Oct through Apr
Water availability: Water available at the Echo Canyon Trailhead
Restrictions: The trailhead is open sunrise to sunset. Entrance gate is locked at night. No parking allowed on streets near the trailhead; vehicles parked in violation of posted signs will be towed; vehicles idling on roads near the trailhead will be ticketed. The trailhead offers restrooms, benches, and a shade ramada. Dogs and pets are prohibited at the trailhead and on the trail. No mountain bikes or horses.
Maps: USGS Paradise Valley; Phoenix Parks website
Trail contact: Phoenix Parks and Recreation Department (see appendix)

Finding the trailhead: Access the trail from the Echo Canyon parking lot on the northwest corner of Camelback Mountain in Echo Canyon Recreation Area. From I-17, take the Glendale exit (#205). Drive east on Glendale Avenue past Piestewa Peak Parkway (AZ 51). Here Glendale Avenue becomes Lincoln Drive. Continue east on Lincoln to Tatum Boulevard. Turn south on Tatum and drive to McDonald Drive. Turn left on McDonald and drive 0.1 mile to a roundabout. Take the second right turn signed "Echo Canyon Trailhead Park" and drive

0.1 mile south to the trailhead and parking lot (GPS: 33.521508, -111.974038). Street address: 4925 E. McDonald Dr.

Parking is problematic on busy days. The trailhead parking lot with seventy-one parking spots and five accessible spots is often filled. Additional parking is available on both sides of the park entrance road past the gatehouse (602-534-5867). Park only in designated areas. Police will ticket all parking offenders.

The Hike

Camelback Mountain, towering above Phoenix and Scottsdale, is a well-known and prominent landmark. The 2,704-foot peak, the highest point in the Phoenix Mountains, is a two-summited mountain that looks like a kneeling camel to the imaginative eye. The higher, eastern summit forms the camel's hump, while the Head is the lower summit to the west. The mountain and its hiking trails are easily accessible, offering a quick getaway that feels far from Phoenix's teeming freeways.

The 1.2-mile (one-way) Echo Canyon Trail, one of the most popular hikes in the area, is a steep, well-maintained path that climbs to the summit of Camelback Mountain from the Echo Canyon Trailhead in the northwest corner of the park. The trail gains 1,264 feet from trailhead to summit, making the gradient over 100 feet per 0.1 mile. You should be prepared for rough terrain, scrambling over boulders, negotiating loose rock and gravel, and climbing steep sections with only a handrail for balance. The trail gets hot, especially between May and September. Carry sufficient water to stay hydrated. Two quarts would not be too much on a hot day. A drinking fountain and restrooms are located at the trailhead. Allow two hours to hike to the summit and return to the parking lot.

Start the hike at the Echo Canyon Trailhead at Echo Canyon parking lot. A shade ramada, interpretive kiosk, and drinking fountain are here. The trail heads uphill into Echo Canyon, a shallow draw flanked by rounded cliffs. Large boulders, tumbled from high cliffs, scatter across the hillsides. Note the Praying Monk, a blocky tower perched on a high terrace above the trail.

At the top of Echo Canyon, stop at an overlook to study Camelback Mountain's geology. The camel's hump and mountain summit to the left are composed of ancient granite approximately 1.5 billion years old. The massive red cliffs to the south are what geologists call the Camel's Head Formation, a 15-million-year-old sedimentary layer divided into four distinctive members. The Papago Park member, which forms the Praying Monk, is a reddish sandstone that was deposited by streams that meandered across an alluvial fan. The rock is alternately layered with coarse beds of cobbles, sand, and silt.

The trail bends south beneath the towering east face of the Hump. A fence lines the trail's left side below the cliff to keep loose rock from tumbling onto houses below. A couple steep sections climbing bare rock are equipped with a handrail for balance. Past the cliff is a trail junction. A short hike west on a spur trail here leads to the camel's neck and views across Phoenix.

The hardest hike segment begins here. The trail climbs steeply up boulder-choked gullies and along airy ridges to a final rocky ravine that leads to Camelback's summit, the hike's halfway point. Use caution on this trail section. Footing is sometimes precarious, with loose boulders and gravel underfoot.

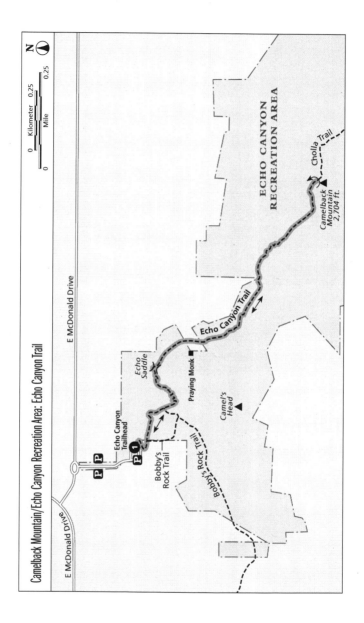

Camelback Mountain/Echo Canyon Recreation Area: Echo Canyon Trail

The rocky summit yields dramatic 360-degree views of Phoenix. To the east rise the distant Superstition and Usery Mountains. The McDowell Mountains and Four Peaks rise to the northeast. To the northwest rises prominent Piestewa Peak. After relaxing on the summit, retrace your steps back to the parking lot. The views are just as good on the way down, and you're not breathing as hard.

Miles and Directions

0.0 Start at the Echo Canyon Trailhead at the west side of the parking lot (GPS: 33.521330, -111.973446). Follow the trail east up a valley hemmed by rounded domes on the left and towering cliffs on the right.

0.3 Reach an overlook at Echo Saddle at the top of Echo Canyon (GPS: 33.520954, -111.970135). Go right and follow the trail south along the base of a cliff. The trail veers away from the cliff and climbs a steep boulder section.

0.6 Reach the hike's marked halfway point and a trail junction on the right (GPS: 33.517697, -111.968341). Keep left and follow the well-worn trail.

1.2 Stand on Camelback Mountain's summit (GPS: 33.514610, -111.961588). After a drink and rest, descend the trail.

2.4 Arrive back at the trailhead (GPS: 33.521329, -111.973443).

2 Camelback Mountain/Echo Canyon Recreation Area: Cholla Trail

The Cholla Trail climbs the long east ridge of 2,704-foot-high Camelback Mountain to 360-degree views across Phoenix and Scottsdale.

Distance: 3.0 miles
Hiking time: 1–3 hours
Type of hike: Out and back
Trail name: Cholla Trail
Difficulty: Strenuous due to steepness and technical terrain. Cumulative elevation gain is 1,320 feet.
Best season: Oct through Apr
Water availability: Drinking water and restrooms at the trailhead

Restrictions: Trailhead and park open 6 a.m. to 7:30 p.m. from May 1 to Sept 30; open 7 a.m. to 5:30 p.m. from Oct 1 to Apr 30. No pets or mountain bikes.
Maps: USGS Paradise Valley; Phoenix Parks website
Trail contact: Phoenix Parks and Recreation Department (see appendix)

Finding the trailhead: The easiest way to the Cholla Trailhead from I-17 is to take the Glendale exit (#205). Turn east on Glendale Avenue and drive to Piestewa Peak Parkway (AZ 51). Here Glendale Avenue turns into Lincoln Drive. Continue east on Lincoln to North Invergordon Road and turn right (south). Park in a designated strip on the west side of North Invergordon Road south of the trailhead next to the Phoenician Resort golf course (GPS: 33.511163, -111.943373). Parking is limited along the road. Parking is often a problem on weekends. There is no parking on East Cholla Lane or Invergordon Road to the north.

To start the hike, walk north on Invergordon Road from the parking strip for 0.1 mile to the signed Cholla Trailhead at a gate (GPS: 33.511380, -111.943530). Trailhead street address: 5150 N Invergordon Rd., Paradise Valley.

The Hike

The 1.5-mile Cholla Trail is a great alternative hike to the steeper and busier Echo Canyon Trail, which climbs the opposite side of Camelback Mountain. The trail gains over 1,300 feet from trailhead to summit, roughly following the mountain's east ridge, and offers stupendous views of Phoenix, Scottsdale, and the Phoenician Resort. Expect steep, rocky sections near the top with scrambling over boulders and along the ridge crest.

No water is available along the trail. Carry plenty to drink, especially in hot weather. A quart or two per person would not be too much. Wear a hat and use sunscreen since the trail bakes in the sun all day. Expect extreme conditions on Camelback, especially on hot days. Turn around if you're overheated to avoid sunstroke and heat exhaustion. Also, stay on the trail. Accidents happen every year to off-trail hikers who fall.

The trail begins north of the Phoenician Resort golf course at a trailhead by North Invergordon Road. Walk west on a sidewalk and through a metal gate. The trail switchbacks up the lower ridge to a scenic overlook with a couple large boulders. The resort, with swimming pools and green fairways, spreads below, while the rocky lumps of Papago Park rise to the south.

The zigzagging trail winds west up a broad ridge, passing saguaro cacti growing among dark boulders, to a rest stop. The ridge rises west of here, while the trail angles right onto the shaded north slope. Follow the rising trail across steep slopes to a saddle with open views.

The last leg climbs an exhilarating, rocky ridge to Camelback Mountain's summit. This section requires boulder

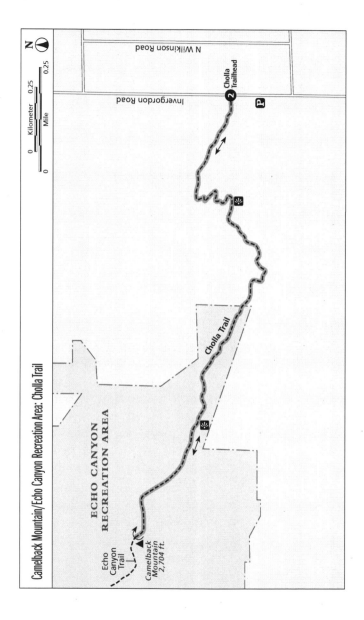

Camelback Mountain/Echo Canyon Recreation Area: Cholla Trail

ECHO CANYON
RECREATION AREA

Echo Canyon Trail

Camelback Mountain
2,704 ft.

Cholla Trail

Cholla Trailhead

N Wilkinson Road

Invergordon Road

N

Kilometer   0.25
0
Mile   0.25
0

hopping and rock scrambling in places, with the mountain slopes dropping steeply away. The ancient granite bedrock offers a rough surface that provides good traction as well as handholds on the steeper sections. Use care when ascending and descending the rocky sections and watch for loose gravel on top of the bedrock.

After the final boulders, the trail ends on the peak's craggy summit. After catching your breath, enjoy panoramic views of Phoenix and surrounding mountain ranges including Piestewa Peak and Mummy Mountain. To the east spreads green fields on the Salt River Pima-Maricopa Indian Community, home of the Onk Akimel O'odham and the Xalychidom Piipaash, and beyond rise the Usery and fabled Superstition Mountains. Afterward, return down the trail to the trailhead.

For an alternative return hike, descend Echo Canyon Trail down Camelback's west side to Echo Canyon parking lot. Walk 0.3 mile north to the Echo Canyon entrance and turn right, following a sidewalk east on the north side of East McDonald Drive for 1.8 miles to Invergordon Road. Turn south on Invergordon and walk 0.9 miles on a sidewalk back to the parking strip for a 6-mile loop hike.

Miles and Directions

- **0.0** Start at the Cholla Trailhead on Invergordon Road. Go through a gate and hike west on a wide trail.
- **0.4** Stop at boulders and an overlook above Phoenician Resort.
- **1.1** Reach a viewpoint above Scottsdale (GPS: 33.512532, -111.956932).
- **1.4** Arrive at the upper saddle (GPS: 33.514465, -111.959982). Continue up the rocky ridge.

1.5 Reach the rocky summit of Camelback Mountain (GPS: 33.514610, -111.961588). Hike back down the trail.

3.0 Arrive back at the trailhead (GPS: 33.511380, -111.943530).

3 Piestewa Peak Recreation Area: Summit Trail

Offering spacious views, Arizona's most popular trail climbs steeply to the rock-rimmed summit of 2,608-foot-high Piestewa Peak.

Distance: 2.4 miles
Hiking time: 1–3 hours
Type of hike: Out and back
Trail name: Piestewa Peak Summit Trail #300
Difficulty: Strenuous due to steepness and technical terrain. Elevation gain is 1,190 feet.
Best season: Oct through Apr
Water availability: No water available on the trail; water available at the ramada by the trailhead
Restrictions: Trailhead hours from 5 a.m. to 7 p.m. Trail hours from 5 a.m. to 11 p.m. Summer hours are in effect from June 1 through Sept 30 at the Piestewa Peak Trailhead. The trailhead parking lot entrance is open until 9 p.m. Piestewa Peak is closed to hikers on days with high heat warnings from 11 a.m. to 5 p.m. No glass containers. To avoid damaging fragile desert ecosystems, do not leave the trail. No pets (dogs) or mountain bikes.
Maps: USGS Sunnyslope; Phoenix Parks website
Trail contact: Phoenix Parks and Recreation Department (see appendix)

Finding the trailhead: From I-17, take the Glendale exit (#205) and drive 4.3 miles east on Glendale Avenue to 0.2 mile past Piestewa Peak Parkway (AZ 51). Here Glendale Avenue turns into Lincoln Drive and bends right. Drive 0.3 mile and take a left turn onto Piestewa Peak Drive. Drive 0.7 mile through a neighborhood into the park. Make the first left turn, signed Mesquite, to the Piestewa Peak Trailhead and two large parking lots (GPS: 33.539585,

-112.022928); street address: 4135 Piestewa Peak Dr. If those lots are filled, park in one of the upper parking lots. The trailhead is behind a ramada on the north side of the first parking lot (GPS: 33.539611, -112.023177).

The Hike

Piestewa Peak, dominating Phoenix's northern skyline, is the centerpiece of the Phoenix Mountains Park and Recreation Area. Many trails lace the 9,000-acre parkland, but none is more revered and popular than the 1.2-mile Piestewa Peak Summit Trail. This steep trail, trod by over half a million hikers annually, attracts more hikers than any other Phoenix trail and is second in Arizona only to the Grand Canyon's Bright Angel Trail in popularity.

This favorite trail, designated a National Recreation Trail in 1974, is packed with hikers and runners on weekends and evenings. The price of this popularity is serious erosion problems that prompted the parks department to pave damaged sections with a mixture of concrete and stone. The peak, formerly named Squaw Peak, was renamed in memory of Lori Piestewa, a Hopi woman and soldier killed in Iraq in 2003. The native Tohono O'odham people call it Vianom Do'ag, meaning "Iron Mountain." Note that trails have numbers as well as names for this hike and many others in this book (numbers are shown in parentheses).

Piestewa Peak is one of the shortest and most strenuous of the day hikes in the Phoenix area. Like neighboring Camelback Mountain, the trail gains 1,200 feet in 1.2 miles or 100 feet every tenth of a mile. Most adults in reasonable physical condition can reach the summit in about an hour of uphill plodding, with a few well-earned rests along the way. However, some fitness buffs breeze past you on the switchbacks, racing to the top in about twenty minutes. Other Phoenicians use the trail as training for a Grand Canyon rim-to-rim trek, working up to four round-trip ascents daily with a loaded pack.

To enjoy your ascent, particularly if you're from out of town and unused to hot temperatures, take your time, take regular rest breaks, and enjoy the views, wear a hat, use sunscreen, and carry water and sports drinks on hot days. There is no shade or water along the trail. Parking is a problem on weekends and in the evening. Plan your hike for other times when the trail is less frequently used.

The Summit Trail (#300) begins at a ramada at the first parking lot on the left after you enter the park. The trailhead is also reached by a short segment of the Freedom Trail from the upper parking areas to the north. The path works up gradual switchbacks to a ridgeline. The Alternate Summit Trail joins the main trail here on the left. This makes a good return path on the descent.

The trail continues up the ridge, steeply switchbacking as it gains elevation. After scrambling up a couple switchbacks, pass rock outcroppings on the ridge crest and reach a junction with Freedom Trail (#302). This excellent loop hike (Hike 5) traverses the circumference of Piestewa Peak. At this intersection you're halfway up the peak and have gained 500 feet of elevation. It's a good place to stop and have a look at the sun-blasted landscape. Other than cigar-shaped saguaros and fishhook barrel cacti, few plants survive on these arid slopes, where surface temperatures can exceed 150°F in summer.

Above here, the trail climbs six switchbacks in a tenth of a mile, crosses to the northwest flank of the ridge, and reaches the only tree on the trail—a palo verde. The trail wraps up the shattered ridge, passing from one side to the other and offering scenic views to valleys below. Occasional railings, installed when this was a horse trail, line a few drop-offs. Piestewa Peak is composed of ancient, billion-year-old schist. This distinctive gray and black rock began as a sedimentary rock subjected to eons of heat and pressure that altered its composition, before it was uplifted and shaped by surface erosion.

The trail's grade steepens for the final section to the summit pyramid. Finish by marching up stone steps to a final scramble up exposed rock outcrops. Go left to the 2,280-foot North Summit or right to the higher 2,608-foot South Summit. It's easier to reach the North Summit first and then follow a lower, less-exposed path for 75 feet across ledges to the South Summit.

Phoenix unfolds below this lofty sky platform with a stunning 360-degree view. Phoenicians readily recognize the surrounding mountain ranges: the ragged Superstitions to the east, the Four Peaks and McDowell Mountains on the northeast horizon, North Mountain to the northwest, and South Mountain topped with antennas to the south. On a clear day, look for the Santa Catalina Mountains by Tucson, 100 miles to the southeast. Camelback Mountain, another popular urban peak that is 30 feet higher than Piestewa Peak, rises to the southeast. Enjoy the view and drink water—you've earned it.

The return hike is all downhill. Take care on the steps and watch for loose gravel. Remember to yield to uphill hikers; trail courtesy dictates that they have the right-of-way. For a different return path, look for the Alternate Summit Trail on the ridge before the final descent to the parking area. This short, 0.33-mile trail angles right and descends a gully and

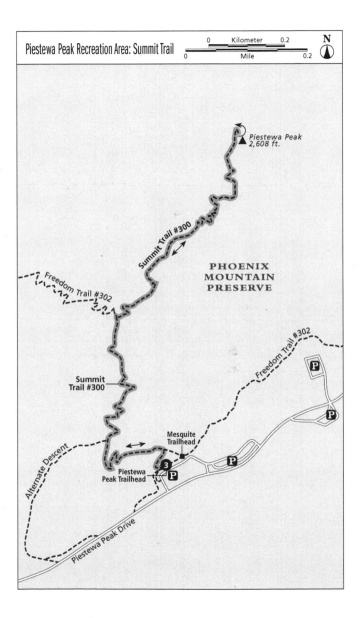

Piestewa Peak Recreation Area: Summit Trail

0 Kilometer 0.2

0 Mile 0.2

N

Piestewa Peak
2,608 ft.

Summit Trail #300

Freedom Trail #302

PHOENIX
MOUNTAIN
PRESERVE

Freedom Trail #302

Summit
Trail #300

Alternate Descent

Mesquite
Trailhead

3

Piestewa
Peak Trailhead

Piestewa Peak Drive

then contours around the lower ridge before climbing back to the parking lot.

Miles and Directions

0.0 Start at the Piestewa Peak Trailhead at a ramada off Piestewa Peak Drive. Hike uphill and join the Piestewa Peak and Freedom Trails. Go left and angle across the mountainside to three steep switchbacks with rock steps.

0.33 Reach a junction at a saddle on a ridge with the Alternate Summit Trail on the left (GPS: 33.540267, -112.024783). Keep straight on the main trail and hike up eight switchbacks, then follow a steep ridge and contour across its right side.

0.6 Reach a junction with Freedom Trail (#302) on the ridge (GPS: 33.543148, -112.024540). Continue straight on Summit Trail and hike steeply along the mountain's rocky south ridge, including a section with thirteen switchbacks. Catch a breather above the switchbacks and then tackle the final section up a groove to the north summit (GPS: 33.547625, -112.021243). Most hikers stop here.

1.2 Scramble across ledges from the north summit to reach the higher south summit of Piestewa Peak (GPS: 33.547390, -112.020920). Enjoy views and then return down the trail.

2.4 Arrive back at the trailhead (GPS: 33.539586, -112.023159).

4 Piestewa Peak Recreation Area: Nature Trail

This fine loop allows hikers to encounter desert plants and animals on the northeast flank of Piestewa Peak and offers scenic views across Phoenix.

Distance: 1.4 miles
Hiking time: About 1 hour
Type of hike: Loop
Trail name: Nature Trail (#304)
Difficulty: Strenuous with steep, technical terrain. Cumulative elevation gain is 370 feet.
Best season: Oct through Apr
Water availability: Drinking water and restrooms available at the trailhead
Restrictions: Open sunrise to sunset. Trailhead hours from 5 a.m. to 7 p.m. Trail hours from 5 a.m. to 11 p.m. Summer hours are in effect from June 1 through Sept 30 at the Piestewa Peak Trailhead. The trailhead parking lot entrance is open until 9 p.m. Pets must be leashed. Dogs are not allowed on trails if temperatures exceed 100°F; violators are punished by fines and possible jail time. No glass containers. To avoid damaging fragile desert ecosystems, do not leave the trail.
Maps: USGS Sunnyslope; Phoenix Parks website
Trail contact: Phoenix Parks and Recreation Department (see appendix)

Finding the trailhead: From I-17, take the Glendale exit (#205) and drive 4.3 miles east on Glendale Avenue to 0.2 mile past Piestewa Peak Parkway (AZ 51). Here Glendale Avenue turns into Lincoln Drive and bends right. Drive 0.3 mile and take a left turn onto Piestewa Peak Drive. Drive through a neighborhood into the park. Continue past the Piestewa Peak Trailhead to the end of the road and a circular parking lot after 1.1 miles (GPS: 33.542705, -112.015532).

Address: 2701 Piestewa Peak Dr. Start the hike at the 304 Trailhead on the parking lot's north side (GPS: 33.542874, -112.015312).

The Hike

Don't let the trail name fool you. This is not a regular "nature trail" by any stretch of the imagination; instead, it's an excellent, clockwise, 1.4-mile loop hike that explores the unique Sonoran Desert ecosystem and quiet valleys and rocky hills east of Piestewa Peak. This well-defined trail makes a fun getaway for hikers searching for a quick hiking fix.

Begin the Nature Trail (#304) at the 304 Trailhead right of the information board on the north side of the parking area. Descend into a deep wash, then scramble up the opposite side and hike north to a junction with Freedom Trail (#302). Continue north alongside a deep ravine tangled with palo verde trees.

The trail climbs toward a saddle. Piestewa Peak looms to the west, its eastern slopes broken by dark cliffs of metamorphic schist and basalt. Tall saguaros nestle in steep draws on the mountainside and cliffs guard the peak's 2,608-foot summit above.

After a half mile, reach the saddle and enjoy a scenic view south to downtown Phoenix and bulky South Mountain beyond. Note the large outcrops of milky white quartz. This rock was deposited as beach sand, but later metamorphosed by extreme heat and pressure into hard quartz. An unnamed shortcut trail goes right from the saddle and rejoins Nature Trail to the east. Don't take it, but continue hiking straight. The trail rolls across a couple dry washes and reaches another junction. Freedom Trail goes left here, while the Nature Trail heads right.

Follow the Nature Trail and descend east beside a shallow wash. The trail threads across a basin surrounded by ridges that cut off the sights and sounds of the surrounding city. This trail section is peaceful and provides a sense of wildness, tucked in the heart of America's fifth-largest city. Look for buckhorn and teddy bear cholla and a few saguaros on the sunbaked ground. The trail dips across a stony wash and heads along its north edge to a Y-junction with Perl Charles Memorial Trail (#1A).

Go right on the Nature Trail and hike south to a junction with two unnamed trails, including the shortcut trail on the right, and climb south. At a saddle, stop for views of downtown's skyscrapers to the south. The hike's last leg descends rocky slopes, winding past saguaros and ocotillos growing on south-facing slopes. The trail descends a hill, then drops into a deep wash, climbs the opposite bank, and threads across a hillside to the trailhead.

Miles and Directions

0.0 Start at the 304 Trailhead right of an informational sign at the parking lot's north end at the end of Piestewa Peak Drive (GPS: 33.542874, -112.015312). After 30 feet, reach a junction on the right with the return trail. Keep left and descend into a wash, then go right, and climb to a junction.

0.1 Reach a junction with Freedom Trail (GPS: 33.543469, -112.015803). Keep right on Freedom/Nature Trail and hike north on slopes west of a wash.

0.45 Reach a saddle between Piestewa Peak on the left and an unnamed knob on the right (GPS: 33.548518, -112.014737) and an informal junction. Keep left on the main trail and continue north into a broad valley.

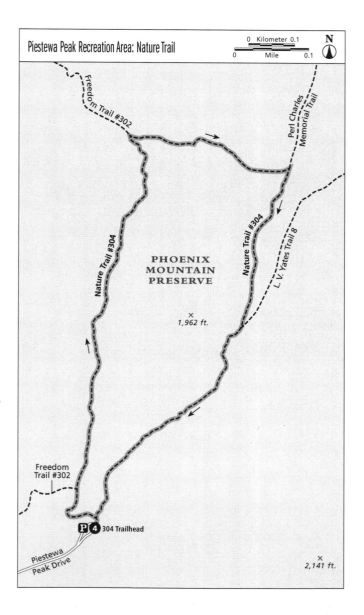

0.6 Reach a junction (GPS: 33.550186, -112.014543). Freedom Trail goes left. Keep right on Nature Trail and hike east down the valley.

0.8 Reach a junction with Perl Charles Memorial Trail (#1A) on the left (GPS: 33.549599, -112.010949). Go right (south) on Nature Trail and hike south on the left side of the rocky knob.

1.05 Meet a junction on the left with L. V. Yates Trail (#8). Keep straight on Nature Trail to a saddle and hike down slopes to the east edge of a wash.

1.4 Arrive back at the trailhead (GPS: 33.542874, -112.015312).

5 Piestewa Peak Recreation Area: Freedom Trail

This excellent moderate hike circumnavigates Piestewa Peak, offering scenic views and solitude.

Distance: 3.7 miles

Hiking time: 2–3 hours

Type of hike: Loop

Trail names: Freedom Trail (#302), Piestewa Peak Summit Trail (#300)

Difficulty: Challenging. Cumulative elevation gain is 1,440 feet.

Best season: Nov through Apr. Summers are hot; get an early start.

Water availability: Drinking water available at the trailhead and picnic area

Restrictions: Trailhead hours from 5 a.m. to 7 p.m. Trail hours from 5 a.m. to 11 p.m. Summer hours are in effect from June 1 through Sept 30 at the Piestewa Peak and Mesquite Trailheads. The trailhead parking lot entrance is open until 9 p.m. Piestewa Peak is closed to hikers on days with high heat warnings from 11 a.m. to 5 p.m. Pets must be leashed, and waste promptly picked up. Dogs are not allowed on trails if temperatures exceed 100°F; violators are punished by fines and possible jail time.

Maps: USGS Sunnyslope topo map (trail not shown); Phoenix Parks website

Trail contact: Phoenix Parks and Recreation Department (see appendix)

Finding the trailhead: From I-17, take the Glendale exit (#205) and drive 4.3 miles east on Glendale Avenue to 0.2 mile past Piestewa Peak Parkway (AZ 51). Here Glendale Avenue turns into Lincoln Drive and bends right. Drive 0.3 mile and take a left turn onto Piestewa Peak Drive. Drive 0.7 mile through a neighborhood into the park. Make the first left turn, signed Mesquite, to the Piestewa Peak and Mesquite Trailheads and two large parking lots (GPS: 33.539585,

-112.022928); street address: 4135 Piestewa Peak Dr. If those lots are filled, park in the upper parking lots. The Mesquite Trailhead (also called the 302 Trailhead) is at a ramada at the first parking lot (GPS: 33.539908, -112.022723).

The Hike

The Freedom Trail (#302) makes a counterclockwise loop hike around 2,608-foot Piestewa Peak. This excellent hike, one of the best in the Phoenix Mountains, offers solitude and gorgeous scenery in the middle of urban Phoenix. While streams of hikers trample the Summit Trail, one of Arizona's most popular hikes, the longer Freedom Trail sees less foot traffic. Like most Phoenix hikes, the trail offers little shade so carry plenty of water and sports drinks and wear a hat on hot days. Restrooms and drinking water are at the trailhead, as well as at other parking lots up the park road.

Begin at the Mesquite Trailhead at a ramada on the right side of the first parking lot. Walk up the trail from the ramada to a junction and go right on Freedom Trail. Going straight is the return trail and the start of the Summit Trail, which climbs to Peistewa Peak's summit. The first segment contours northeast below the steep south-facing slopes of Piestewa Peak. Walk up the stony path, with the road and ramadas to your right to a junction with Nature Trail and go left. The Freedom and Nature Trails share the next segment.

Hike north below the eastern flank of Piestewa Peak, its summit guarded by dark cliffs composed of metamorphic rock. The trail climbs alongside a deep ravine filled with palo verde trees, the Arizona state tree, to a broad saddle east of the peak. Catch your breath and look south toward Phoenix's skyscraper skyline and distant South Mountain topped with an array of antennas.

Past the saddle the trail dips across dry washes on the edge of a valley and reaches the intersection of Freedom Trail and Trail 1A, the Perl Charles Memorial Trail. The Nature and Perl Charles Memorial Trails go right. Keep left on Freedom Trail, which shares the next hike leg with the Perl Charles Memorial Trail.

Next is the hike's hardest section, which climbs to a pass north of Piestewa Peak. The trail switchbacks up steep slopes to the skyline 2,120-foot saddle. Dark cliffs rear above, revealing saguaros tucked into rocky ravines. A couple benches at the saddle let you rest and enjoy marvelous views of North Mountain, Shaw Butte, and Lookout Mountain.

From the saddle, descend four switchbacks to a deep canyon that drains southwest. The trail follows a ravine and then contours across steep slopes, making a long descent across the peak's west face. Eventually the trail levels as it contours to a gap and a junction with Perl Charles Memorial Trail on the right.

Continue along the mountain's flank, crossing washes to the trail's low point. A rough trail drops right here to a housing development. Make a sharp left turn on Freedom Trail and hike past a palo verde tree. The next section is tough, especially on hot days. Climb steadily uphill for a half mile to the Summit Trail at a gap on Piestewa Peak's south ridge. If you're energetic, take an extra-credit side hike and scramble up Summit Trail to Piestewa Peak's rock-rimmed summit. Finish the hike by descending east to the trailhead on a section shared with the busy Summit Trail.

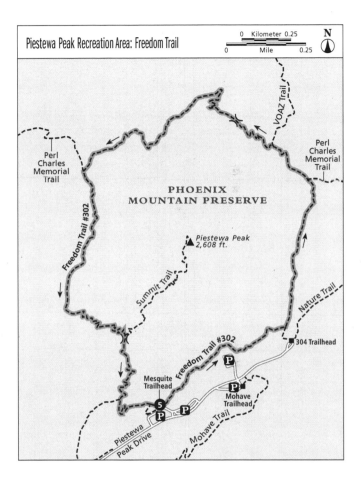

Piestewa Peak Recreation Area: Freedom Trail

0 Kilometer 0.25
0 Mile 0.25

N

VOAZ Trail

Perl
Charles
Memorial
Trail

Perl
Charles
Memorial
Trail

PHOENIX
MOUNTAIN PRESERVE

Freedom Trail #302

Piestewa Peak
2,608 ft.

Summit Trail

Nature Trail

Freedom Trail #302

304 Trailhead

Mesquite
Trailhead

P

P

5
P **P**

Mohave
Trailhead

P

Piestewa
Peak Drive

Mohave Trail

Miles and Directions

0.0 Start at the Mesquite Trailhead on the right side of the first
parking lot. Walk 60 feet up the Freedom/Summit Trails to a
junction and go right on Freedom Trail.

0.6 Reach a junction on the right with Nature Trail (#304) and go left on Freedom/Nature Trails (GPS: 33.543474, -112.015783). Hike north along the west side of a deep ravine.

1.0 Reach a low saddle on the east side of Piestewa Peak. Continue north into a valley.

1.1 Reach a junction on the right with the Nature Trail (GPS: 33.550186, -112.014543). Keep left on Freedom Trail and begin climbing slopes.

1.3 Reach a trail junction on the right with VOAZ Trail (GPS: 33.551687, -112.016480). Keep left on Freedom Trail.

1.5 Climb steeply up switchbacks to a high saddle north of Piestewa Peak. Descend on the trail and contour southwest across Piestewa Peak's lower slopes.

2.3 Reach the junction of Freedom and Perl Charles Memorial Trails (GPS: 33.550589, -112.026713). Go left on Freedom Trail and hike south.

2.75 Arrive below steep slopes (GPS: 33.544233, -112.027699) and climb seventeen switchbacks to a notch on Piestewa Peak.

3.2 Meet the Summit Trail at a junction in a notch on Piestewa Peak's south ridge (GPS: 33.543150, -112.024546).

Extra Credit: Hike 0.6 mile to the peak's summit and then back to the notch for an extra 1.2 miles. Descend the well-traveled trail down steep slopes on the peak's southeast flank.

3.7 Arrive back at the trailhead (GPS: 33.539908, -112.022723).

6 Piestewa Peak Recreation Area: Mohave Trail

Good short nature trail that ends at a scenic viewpoint on Mohave Point above Phoenix.

Distance: 1.2 miles
Hiking time: About 1 hour
Type of hike: Out and back
Trail name: Mohave Trail (#200)
Difficulty: Moderate. Elevation gain is 308 feet.
Best season: Nov through Apr
Water availability: Water available at the picnic area
Restrictions: Trailhead hours from 5 a.m. to 7 p.m. Trail hours from 5 a.m. to 11 p.m. Summer hours are in effect from June 1 through Sept 30. The trailhead parking lot entrance is open until 9 p.m. Pets must be leashed, and waste must be promptly picked up. Dogs are not allowed on trails if temperatures exceed 100°F; violators are punished by fines and possible jail time. No glass containers. To avoid damaging fragile desert ecosystems, do not leave the trail.
Maps: USGS Sunnyslope (trail not shown); Phoenix Parks website
Trail contact: Phoenix Parks and Recreation Department (see appendix)

Finding the trailhead: From I-17, take the Glendale exit (#205) and drive 4.3 miles east on Glendale Avenue to 0.2 miles past Piestewa Peak Parkway (AZ 51). Here Glendale Avenue turns into Lincoln Drive and bends right. Drive 0.3 mile and take a left turn onto Piestewa Peak Drive. Drive 0.9 mile through a neighborhood and the park to a right turn into a parking lot labeled Mohave, four picnic ramadas, and the Mohave Trailhead (GPS: 33.540648, -112.018266). Street address: 5594 Piestewa Peak Dr.

The Hike

The Mohave Trail is a 0.4-mile (one way) trail that ascends a rocky ridge south of Piestewa Peak to the summit of 1,788-foot Mohave Point, which offers a spectacular view of Phoenix and the surrounding mountains. The summit view is especially nice at sunset.

Begin on the east side of the Mohave parking lot at a signed trailhead for Mohave Trail. Walk north through a ramada and follow the trail to the junction of Mohave Trail and Trail #200A. Keep right on Mohave. A large quartz outcrop marks the junction. Brittlebushes, blanketed with yellow blossoms in spring, spill down slopes below the trail.

Contour along the trail on the north flank of a rocky ridge to a narrow saddle. Continue right on the steepening trail which switchbacks up the east face of a peak. Small outcrops of tilted schist and mica rocks scatter across the hillside. When the trail levels, arrive at the 1,788-foot-high summit of Mohave Point, a long rocky ridge.

After scrambling onto the highest point, bask in the sun and take in the spacious view. Piestewa Peak dominates across the canyon above the road. Hikers dot its popular Summit Trail on the south ridge. Phoenix spreads across the broad valley to the south, with the rugged profile of South Mountain and Sierra Estrella forming its southern skyline. Camelback Mountain, the prominent, pyramid-shaped peak, rises to the southeast.

Miles and Directions

0.0 Start at the Mohave Trailhead at the parking lot. Hike north and then south on the steepening trail.

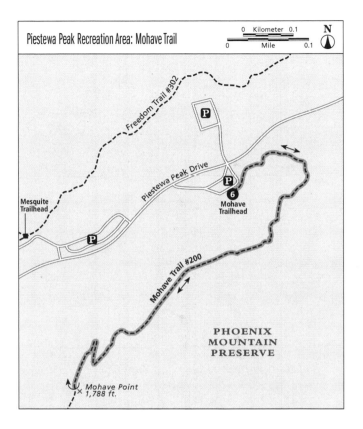

Piestewa Peak Recreation Area: Mohave Trail

0.3 Reach the junction of Mohave Trail and Trail #200A (GPS: 33.539558, -112.018207). Keep right on Mohave Trail.

0.45 Reach a saddle. Climb the steep trail up the north side of a peak.

0.6 Reach the summit of Mohave Point (GPS: 33.537299, -112.021715). Return down the trail.

1.2 Arrive back at the trailhead (GPS: 33.540648, -112.018266).

7 Papago Park: Double Butte Loop Trail

This easy loop hike around sandstone formations in Papago Park makes a great introduction to desert hiking.

Distance: 2.3 miles
Hiking time: 1-2 hours
Type of hike: Loop
Trail name: Double Butte Loop Trail
Difficulty: Easy. Elevation gain of 50 feet.
Best season: Nov through Apr
Water availability: None
Restrictions: Parking, entrance, and trail hours are sunrise to sunset. Hiker-only trail. Pets must be leashed and waste promptly picked up. Dogs are not allowed on trails if temperatures exceed 100°F; violators are punished by fines and possible jail time. No glass bottles. Smoking only inside an enclosed vehicle.
Maps: USGS Tempe (trail not shown); Phoenix Parks website
Trail contact: Phoenix Parks and Recreation Department (see appendix)

Finding the trailhead: Drive west from I-10 on Loop 202/Red Mountain Freeway to Priest Drive exit (#6). Turn north on Priest Drive and head north on Galvin Parkway for 2.3 miles. Turn left (west) on Papago Peak Road opposite the Phoenix Zoo turn on the right. Drive 350 feet and turn right into the large West Buttes Parking Lot. Start at the trailhead on the left side of a ramada on the parking lot's north end (GPS: 33.455331, -111.954412).

The Hike

Papago Park is a 1,496-acre natural reserve in southeast Phoenix. The mostly wild park, originally a Hohokam village and later Papago Saguaro National Monument, offers ten hiking trails, an orienteering course, the Phoenix Municipal Golf Course, picnic areas with ramadas, and the Phoenix

Zoo and Desert Botanical Garden. The park is characterized by several huge humps of sandstone, visible from much of Phoenix. Before it was a park, the area was the site of a World War II prisoner of war camp from 1942 to 1944, housing as many as 3,100 prisoners.

The Double Butte Loop Trail, beginning from a trailhead at West Buttes Parking Lot opposite the Phoenix Zoo, loops around two large sandstone formations. Many social trails thread across the park, so avoid damaging desert vegetation and causing erosion by following the well-traveled trail. Watch out for mountain bikers who also use the trail.

Begin your hike at the trailhead at the ramada on the north side of West Buttes Parking Lot. Follow the gently rising trail north to a junction with Little Butte Loop Trail. For extra credit, go left on Little Butte Loop Trail, which makes an easy half-mile circuit around the smaller central butte. From the junction, continue north, passing William C. Elliot Memorial to Eliot Ramada Loop, a closed paved road, which is the 2.7-mile, wheelchair-accessible Eliot Ramada Loop Trail.

Go right on the road to a junction and head east on Double Butte Loop Trail. The next segment goes around the eastern flank of a massive 1,663-foot-high sandstone dome. Creosote bushes dominate the arid landscape. The trail dips across washes and bends west on the butte's north side, paralleling McDowell Road to the north. Reach the stone steps of Papago Amphitheater at the hike's halfway point. The open-air amphitheater, built in 1933–1934 by the Civilian Conservation Corps, seats 3,500 people and is used for events including Easter sunrise services.

The sandstone formation here, called Camel's Head Formation, also occurs on Camelback Mountain to the north.

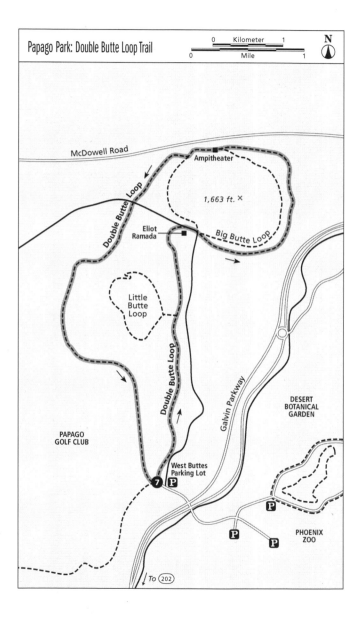

Papago Park: Double Butte Loop Trail

0 Kilometer 1
0 Mile 1

N

McDowell Road

Double Butte Loop

Ampitheater

1,663 ft. ×

Eliot Ramada

Big Butte Loop

Little Butte Loop

Double Butte Loop

PAPAGO GOLF CLUB

Galvin Parkway

DESERT BOTANICAL GARDEN

West Buttes Parking Lot

7 P

P

P

P

PHOENIX ZOO

To 202

Note the huge holes called "tafoni" by geologists. These occur when water seeps into bedrock and dissolves minerals. To see a large tafoni hole after doing this hike, drive on Papago Road to a trailhead north of the Phoenix Zoo and follow paved 0.25-mile Hole in the Rock Trail to the unique Hole in the Rock.

From the amphitheater, continue west and then southwest below the humped formation. The trail heads southwest and crosses Eliot Ramada Loop Trail. From the road, the last segment heads south across slopes sandwiched between Little Butte and Papago Golf Club. Finish at a trailhead on the southwest side of the parking lot.

Miles and Directions

0.0 Begin at the trailhead on the north side of West Buttes Parking Lot opposite the Phoenix Zoo (GPS: 33.455331, -111.954412). Hike north on Double Butte Loop Trail.

0.4 Junction with Little Butte Loop Trail (GPS: 33.460067, -111.953911). Continue straight.

0.6 Reach accessible Eliot Ramada Loop Trail, a closed road (GPS: 33.463100, -111.953510). Go right on the road and walk east for 200 feet. After the road bends right, go left on the trail (GPS: 33.462929, -111.952957).

1.2 Reach Papago Amphitheater north of the butte (GPS: 33.465844, -111.952059). Continue on the trail around the north end of the butte and then hike south below it.

1.4 Reach a junction with paved Eliot Ramada Loop Trail (GPS: 33.464073, -111.955572). Cross the closed road and continue straight on Double Buttes Loop Trail. Hike below smaller buttes alongside the Papago Golf Club.

2.3 Arrive at a trailhead at the southwest corner of the parking lot (GPS: 33.454796, -111.954859).

8 North Mountain Park: North Mountain National Trail

This fun moderate hike traverses 2,104-foot North Mountain, a landmark peak topped with antennas in north Phoenix.

Distance: 1.6 miles

Hiking time: 1–2 hours

Type of hike: Loop

Trail name: North Mountain National Trail

Difficulty: Moderately challenging. Elevation gain is 614 feet.

Best season: Nov through Apr

Water availability: Water and restrooms in the main picnic area south of the trailhead

Restrictions: Trailhead hours from 5 a.m. to 7 p.m. Trail hours from 5 a.m. to 11 p.m. Hiker-only trail. Dogs must be leashed and waste promptly picked up. Dogs are not allowed on trails if temperatures exceed 100°F; violators are punished by fines and possible jail time. Glass containers are prohibited. No specimen collecting or piñatas in the ramadas. To avoid damaging fragile desert ecosystems, do not leave the trail.

Maps: USGS Sunnyslope (trail not shown); Phoenix Parks website

Trail contacts: Phoenix Parks and Recreation Department; North Mountain Visitor Center (see appendix)

Finding the trailhead: From I-17, take the Thunderbird Road exit (#210). Turn east on Thunderbird Road and drive 3.1 miles to 7th Street. Turn right (south) on 7th Street and drive south for 2.2 miles past the east side of North Mountain to Peoria Avenue. Turn right (west) into North Mountain Recreation Area and go right on the park loop road for 0.3 mile to Maricopa Ramada at the loop's north end. Park in the lot here (GPS: 33.585365, -112.066262); 10600 North 7th St. The trailhead is right of the ramada at a sign (GPS:

33.585690, -112.066247). If the parking lot is full, park in one of the other lots in the recreation area and walk to the trailhead.

The Hike

North Mountain, a pyramid-shaped peak northwest of Piestewa Peak, looms over 7th Street in north Phoenix. The 2,104-foot mountain, topped by transmission towers, offers a challenging loop up North Mountain National Trail on its east flank. The well-marked trail is easy to follow, although it is narrow, steep, and rocky on the singletrack descent section. The trail is marked by square metal posts with trail number 44. Be sure to carry enough water, especially when it is hot since the trail bakes in the sun and no shade is found.

The North Mountain National Trailhead is at the north end of the Maricopa Ramada parking lot next to the ramada and trail signs. Hike north on the marked trail up a draw to a saddle. This steep trail section wakes up your legs in a hurry. From the saddle, scramble up steps to paved North Mountain Road. The mile-long road, beginning on 7th Street, is a single-lane service road that provides access to towers on North Mountain's summit. It's closed to vehicle traffic, but open to hikers.

Follow the road up the northeast flank of North Mountain for a half mile. Walking on the paved surface is easy, but the grade is sustained. Overlooks along the way let you catch your breath before continuing upward. Below the cluster of antennas at the summit, the road ends at a scenic viewpoint.

A rocky trail heads up the final slope to the mountain's 2,104-foot summit south of the viewpoint. The actual mountaintop is fenced off, so the trail ends on the ridge south of it. The summit overlook yields spacious views of nearby Shaw Butte, Piestewa Peak, and skyscrapers in downtown Phoenix.

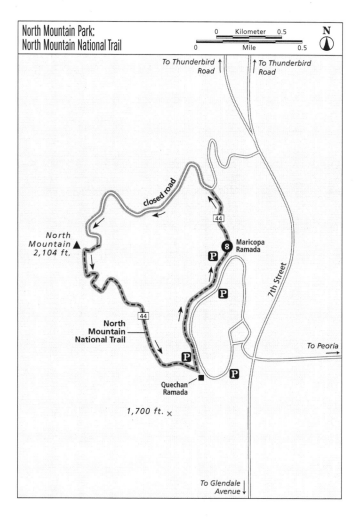

North Mountain Park:
North Mountain National Trail

0 Kilometer 0.5

0 Mile 0.5

N

To Thunderbird Road

To Thunderbird Road

closed road

North Mountain 2,104 ft.

44

Maricopa Ramada

8

P

P

P

7th Street

North Mountain National Trail

44

To Peoria

P

P

Quechan Ramada

1,700 ft. ×

To Glendale Avenue

The descent trail is more exciting than the ascent, with a rough path traversing steep, rocky slopes. From the summit, hike south along the crest of the peak's south ridge. Note an outcropping of white quartz alongside the trail below the summit. Farther down, look for upturned layers of schist. The steep trail descends to a notch on the ridge. Keep left here and follow the switchbacking trail down the mountain's arid east face. Plants scatter across the slope, including ocotillos, palo verde trees, creosote bushes, and bursage shrubs.

From the notch, drop around the west side of the rocky crest. Houses fill a narrow canyon southeast of the trail. At a saddle, reach a three-way trail junction. Go left and descend to Quechan Ramada and the trail's end.

Return to the trailhead by walking north on the paved loop road to the parking lot at Maricopa Ramada. Along the way are a ranger station, restrooms, water, and a playground.

Miles and Directions

0.0 Start at the trailhead right of Maricopa Ramada. Hike north up the steep trail.

0.15 Reach North Mountain Road (GPS: 33.587636, -112.066881) and go left up the road.

0.65 Arrive at North Mountain's summit (GPS: 33.585685, -112.071653). At the end of the pavement, hike south on a trail below the towers onto the peak's south ridge

1.1 Reach a saddle above houses to the west (GPS: 33.581513, -112.069215). Go left on the marked trail.

1.3 Reach a trailhead at Quechan Ramada and the paved park loop road (GPS: 33.581409, -112.067693). Go left and walk up the left side of the road on a marked pedestrian lane.

1.6 Arrive back at the trailhead (GPS: 33.585690, -112.066247).

9 North Mountain Park: Shaw Butte Trail

This rambling loop hike climbs over and around Shaw Butte in the northern Phoenix Mountains.

Distance: 4.0 miles
Hiking time: 2–4 hours
Type of hike: Loop
Trail name: Shaw Butte Trail (#306)
Difficulty: Moderately challenging. Elevation gain is 654 feet.
Best season: Nov through Apr
Water availability: Water available at the trailhead
Restrictions: Trailhead hours from May 1 to Sept 1 5 a.m. to 7 p.m.; Oct 1 to Apr 30 6 a.m. to 7 p.m. Trail hours from 5 a.m. to 11 p.m. Dogs must be leashed, and waste must be picked up. Dogs are not allowed on trails if temperatures exceed 100°F; violators are punished by fines and possible jail time. Glass containers are prohibited. No specimen collecting. To avoid damaging fragile desert ecosystems, do not leave the trail.
Maps: USGS Sunnyslope (trail not shown); Phoenix Parks website
Trail contact: Phoenix Parks and Recreation Department (see appendix)

Finding the trailhead: From I-17, take the Thunderbird Road exit (#210). Drive east on Thunderbird Road for 2.5 miles to Central Avenue. Turn right (south) on Central and drive 0.3 mile to the Shaw Butte Trailhead and parking lot on the right side of the road (GPS: 33.603575, -112.074176). Trailhead address: 12898 North Central Ave. Shaw Butte Trailhead (GPS: 33.603728, -112.074292) is on the west side of the parking area at a gap in a stucco wall.

The Hike

The Shaw Butte Trail offers a scenic loop hike over 2,149-foot Shaw Butte, one of the northernmost summits in the Phoenix Mountains. Shaw Butte and its neighbor North Mountain are both crowned by clusters of towers and antennas. The bulky butte lies east of I-17 in north Phoenix. Square brown posts with trail number 306 and directional arrows mark the trail's route.

Start at the Shaw Butte Trailhead at the parking lot. A kiosk with a map and park information is just beyond it. Head southwest up a closed gravel road that is used to service towers atop Shaw Butte. The road makes a switchback and then follows the peak's broad northeast ridge. Barrel cacti, a few saguaros, and palo verde trees grow among basalt boulders alongside the road.

Higher, the road is paved with rough asphalt, and steadily edges above a huge amphitheater below the butte's summit. The north-facing slopes below the road are moister than south-facing slopes, offering a carpet of bright yellow blossoms of brittlebushes in springtime. Above the road stretch cliff bands of dark basalt, a volcanic rock deposited as an ancient lava flow.

Below the top, the hike reaches a three-way road junction north of the fenced towers and antennas atop the summit. Take a quick jaunt up the left fork to stand on the high point. The hike goes right and descends a narrow road to a saddle between the main summit and a lower summit. At a junction, go left on an old road to barriers blocking the roadway. The trail contours across the butte's southwest face.

The trail reaches the mountain's south ridge and the ruins of swanky Cloud 9 Restaurant. All that remains of the restaurant are concrete foundations and worn pavement. The structure was built in 1958 as a residence, but the owners, Richard and Barbara Barker, opened it as a restaurant in 1961. A giant neon "9," perched atop a 50-foot-high steel pole, advertised its mountaintop aerie. Every evening Richard shuttled diners up a narrow paved road in a Land Rover or Mercury Voyager station wagon on the mountain's south flank to the restaurant, where they supped on steaks and seafood and enjoyed magnificent nighttime views of Phoenix. The restaurant burned down on November 8, 1964.

The next section can be confusing. Watch for brown marker posts to stay on track. Descend a rocky road that contours onto the mountain's south side. Follow switchbacks down the south ridge to a junction. Leave the road and go left on the trail to another old road section and another junction. Go left on a singletrack trail and descend switchbacks to a sloping apron.

Continue east to a junction and hike to an obvious gap in a ridge. Descend sharply into the wide valley between Shaw Butte and North Mountain. Keep right at a Y-junction below the gap and reach Christiansen Trail (#100). Turn left on Shaw Butte Trail and hike north to the trailhead.

Miles and Directions

0.0 Start at the Shaw Butte Trailhead on the parking lot's northwest side (GPS: 33.603732, -112.074300). Hike west to a junction.

0.1 Reach a junction and the start of the Shaw Butte Trail (#306) loop. Go straight and hike west up the closed road/trail, bending around the butte's north flank and then following the trail up the western slope of its north ridge. The return trail is left of the junction.

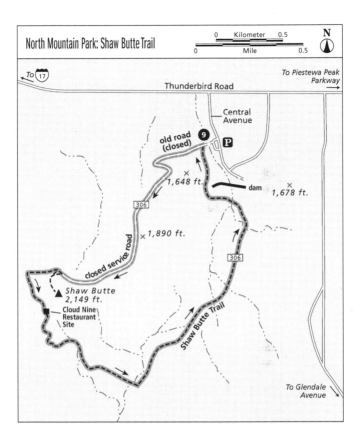

North Mountain Park: Shaw Butte Trail

1.3 Reach a three-way junction below the summit (GPS: 33.595467, -112.086589). Continue straight on the old road. To tag the high point, go left to the summit's antenna field.

1.45 Reach a junction at a saddle on the southwest side of Shaw Butte (GPS: 33.595360, -112.089391). Go left on an old road and hike south past the Cloud 9 Restaurant ruins on the left.

1.85 Reach a road/trail junction on the south ridge (GPS: 33.589855, -112.087586). Go left on the trail and hike east down an old road.

1.9 Reach another junction with the road going right. Go left on singletrack Shaw Butte Trail and descend seven switchbacks in a steep gully. Continue down slopes past a junction before a wash and then hike east past more social trail junctions to a saddle. On the east side of the saddle, keep right on the trail and descend to a wash in a valley.

2.5 Climb out of the wash and reach a major signed junction with Christiansen Trail (#100) (GPS: 33.587918, -112.079848). Turn left on Shaw Butte Trail (shared with Christiansen Trail for next 0.2 mile) and hike north.

2.7 Reach a Y-junction with Shaw Butte Trail going left and Christiansen Trail going right (GPS: 33.590567, -112.077860). Go left on Shaw Butte Trail, dip across a couple washes, and hike north past a couple junctions on the right with connector trails to Christiansen Trail.

3.7 Reach a junction with a connector trail on the right just before an earthen levee; keep left on Shaw Butte Trail.

3.9 Reach the first junction at the start of Shaw Butte Trail. Go right and hike east toward the parking lot.

4.0 Arrive back at the trailhead (GPS: 33.603728, -112.074292).

10 Lookout Mountain Park: Summit Trail

A short moderate hike climbs to a scenic viewpoint atop rock-rimmed Lookout Mountain.

Distance: 1.0 mile
Hiking time: About 1 hour
Type of hike: Out and back
Trail name: Lookout Mountain Summit Trail (#150)
Difficulty: Moderate. Elevation gain is 475 feet.
Best season: Nov through Apr
Water availability: Water available at the trailhead
Restrictions: Parking and entrance hours sunrise to 7 p.m. or sunset (whichever comes first). Trail hours from 5 a.m. to 11 p.m. Hiker-only trail; no mountain bikes. Dogs must be leashed and pet waste picked up. Dogs are not allowed on trails if temperatures exceed 100°F; violators are punished by fines and possible jail time. Glass containers are prohibited. No specimen collecting. To avoid damaging fragile desert ecosystems, do not leave the trail.
Maps: USGS Sunnyslope and Union Hills (trail not shown); Phoenix Parks website
Trail contacts: Phoenix Parks and Recreation Department; North Mountain Visitor Center (see appendix)

Finding the trailhead: Drive north from downtown Phoenix on I-17 to Bell Road exit 212. Turn east on Bell Road and drive 3.8 miles to 16th Street. Turn right onto 16th Street and drive south past Greenway Parkway for 0.8 mile to a parking lot and the Lookout Mountain Trailhead at the road's end (GPS: 33.627052, -112.048331). Trailhead address: 15600 North 16th St. The gate at the parking lot entrance is open from sunrise to 7 p.m. or sunset (whichever comes first).

The Hike

The 0.5-mile Summit Trail, offering lofty views across north Phoenix, scrambles to the spacious summit of 2,054-foot Lookout Mountain. The trail has both gentle and steep grades and a few rocky sections. Allow an hour to ascend and descend the peak. Carry water since the trail is hot and no shade is found. Drinking water is at the trailhead.

The Lookout Mountain Trailhead is at the south end of the parking lot. Walk past a park map and a warning sign to a brown post signed for the Summit Trail and the Circumference Trail (#308). Hike up the rocky trail to another post that marks the junction of the two trails. Go left on Summit Trail.

Head southeast up the trail to switchbacks that zigzag up the mountain's steep north flank. Pass another signpost below a cliff band composed of basalt, a volcanic rock. Contour west along the base of the cliffs and scramble to a saddle between Lookout Mountain's east and west summits. A quick climb west leads to the lower 1,964-foot west summit.

From the saddle, hike east and scramble up loose, broken rock to a ridge. Follow the easy ridge to Lookout Mountain's flat, 2,054-foot east summit. A brown post marks the high point. From here, enjoy a 360-degree vista of Phoenix and the surrounding mountain ranges.

Look to the northwest at the bulky Bradshaw Mountains. The McDowell Mountains and pointed Pinnacle Peak straddle the eastern horizon. Beyond looms the Four Peaks, the Phoenix Mountains, including Piestewa Peak, the skyline of downtown Phoenix, and South Mountain to the south. After taking in the view, backtrack down the trail to the parking lot.

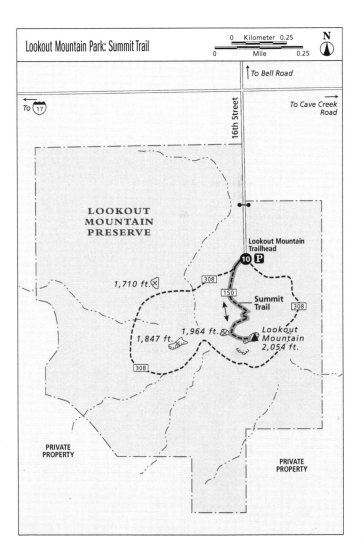

Lookout Mountain Park: Summit Trail

To Bell Road

To 17

To Cave Creek Road

16th Street

LOOKOUT
MOUNTAIN
PRESERVE

Lookout Mountain
Trailhead

10 P

1,710 ft.

308

150

Summit
Trail

308

1,847 ft.

1,964 ft.

Lookout
Mountain
2,054 ft.

308

PRIVATE
PROPERTY

PRIVATE
PROPERTY

N

Kilometer 0.25

Mile 0.25

Miles and Directions

0.0 Start at the Lookout Mountain Trailhead on the southwest corner of the parking lot. Hike southwest up the signed, stony trail.

0.1 Reach the junction of trails #150 and #308; go left on the Summit Trail #150.

0.3 Reach a saddle between the mountain's east and west summits (GPS: 33.623622, -112.049262). Go left on the signed rocky trail and climb to the east summit.

0.5 Arrive at the summit of Lookout Mountain (GPS: 33.623324, -112.047326).

1.0 Arrive back at the trailhead (GPS: 33.627052, -112.048331).

11 Phoenix Sonoran Preserve: Union Peak Loop

This excellent loop hike, following several trail segments, traverses a pristine desert environment and climbs to the summit of Union Peak.

Distance: 6.6 miles

Hiking time: 2–3 hours

Type of hike: Loop

Trail names: Hawk's Nest Trail, Dixie Mountain Loop, Valle Vista Trail, Great Horned Owl Trail, Union Peak Trail, Desert Tortoise Trail

Difficulty: Moderate with easy grades. Elevation gain is 650 feet.

Best season: Oct through Apr

Water availability: None

Restrictions: Trailhead open sunrise to sunset. Gate is locked at night. Dogs must be leashed and waste picked up. Dogs are not allowed on trails if temperatures exceed 100°F; violators are punished by fines and possible jail time.

Maps: USGS Union Hills; Phoenix Parks website

Trail contact: Phoenix Parks and Recreation Department (see appendix)

Finding the trailhead: Reach the trailhead from I-17 in north Phoenix. Take Jomax Road exit (#219) and turn east on West Jomax Road. Drive east on West Jomax and drive 1.1 miles to North Valley Parkway and turn left or north on it. Drive north on the parkway for 0.9 mile to West Copperhead Trail. Turn right or northeast on West Copperhead and drive one block, then turn left on North Melvern Trail. Drive two blocks and turn right on Desert Vista Trail and follow to the parking lot and the Desert Vista Trailhead (GPS: 33.741152, -112.097244). Trailhead address: 1900 Desert Vista Trail.

The Hike

This wonderful hike, following six different trail segments, explores the Phoenix Sonoran Preserve, an area of wilderness north of Phoenix and east of I-17. The rugged preserve, encompassing the Union Hills, currently includes over 9,000 acres in two large parcels; the master plan calls for an eventual land total exceeding 20,000 acres.

The preserve's southern sector offers 13.6 miles of hiking on eleven trails that explore the Union Hills. The well-constructed trails are wide, have gentle grades, are well marked, and are easy to follow. The described hike threads around Dixie Mountain, crosses broad Valle Vista, climbs to the summit of Union Peak, and then returns to the trailhead. It can be easily shortened by chopping out the Union Peak segment. All junctions are well marked with signs.

Besides great hiking, the preserve is excellent for wildflower watching in spring—March and April—as well as for wildlife observation. Watch for rattlesnakes during the warmer months. Remember to carry plenty of water since the sun is hot and little shade is found along the trails.

Begin at the Desert Vista Trailhead at the end of Desert Vista Trail on the edge of a neighborhood. Hike northeast up Hawk's Nest Trail, crossing a scrubby hillside to its junction with Desert Tortoise Trail. Keep left on Hawk's Nest. Desert Tortoise is the return trail for the hike.

Past the junction, look up left to a tall six-armed saguaro. Note a large nest of twigs and branches in the crook of the saguaro—this is the hawk's nest the trail is named after. In springtime, a great horned owl takes up residence in the nest. Keep an eye out for a nest of fuzzy white owlets in late March.

The trail continues uphill to a saddle and junction with Dixie Mountain Loop Trail marked with a brown post. Go right on Dixie Mountain Loop, designated with a "D" on the post. The next segment traverses slopes studded with cacti, creosote bushes, brittlebush, ocotillos, and palo verde trees. The hike reaches another trail junction on the east flank of 2,277-foot Dixie Mountain. Go right here on Valle Vista Trail (marked "V" on brown post).

The trail descends gravelly slopes to a broad bajada or outwash plain. Saguaro cacti, some multiarmed and some cigar-shaped, line the trail. After descending from the last junction, the hike reaches a major junction with Desert Tortoise Trail. For a shorter hike—3.1 miles total—go right or south on Desert Tortoise Trail, which returns to Hawk's Nest Trail and the trailhead.

The rest of the hike travels from this junction to the summit of Union Peak and back for an additional 3 miles, offering spectacular views from the mountaintop. From the junction, continue straight on Valle Vista Trail to its junction with Cactus Wren Trail, which goes left. Continue straight on Valle Vista and climb to a low saddle and three-way trail junction. Valle Vista Trail ends here, and 3.1-mile Great Horned Owl Trail, a loop around Union Mountain, begins.

Go left and hike east on Great Horned Owl Trail. The trail ascends a blunt ridgeline and then gently climbs across the northwestern slope of Union Peak to a trail junction and brown post. Go right, following the arrow on the post for "UP."

From the junction, the trail climbs and switchbacks across the mountain's north face, gaining almost 550 feet from junction to the top. Eventually the trail emerges onto a false summit. Continue south along a ridge and a half mile from the junction, reach the 2,383-foot summit of Union Peak. Sit on the summit rocks and sign your name in the summit register.

After a rest, retrace the trails back to the junction of Valle Vista and Desert Tortoise Trails in the flat between Dixie Mountain and Union Mountain. Go left or southwest on Desert Tortoise Trail. The trail edges below mountains, dipping across washes and crossing slopes covered with cacti and scrubby brush. From the last wash, climb to a final junction with Hawk's Nest Trail and rejoin the first trail segment. Go left and hike downhill to the trailhead.

Miles and Directions

0.0 Start at the Desert Vista Trailhead. Go north on Hawk's Nest Trail.

0.3 Reach a trail junction with Desert Tortoise Trail (GPS: 33.743321, -112.094538). Go left up hill on Hawk's Nest Trail.

0.5 Meet a trail junction and the end of Hawk's Nest Trail (GPS: 33.744888, -112.092996). Go right or northeast on Dixie Mountain Loop Trail.

0.9 Reach the junction of Dixie Mountain Loop and Valle Vista Trail (GPS: 33.747373, -112.087072). Go right and hike downhill on Valle Vista Trail.

1.4 Reach a wide valley floor with a cacti garden.

1.7 Reach a junction with Desert Tortoise Trail (GPS: 33.742646, -112.081988). Continue straight on Valle Vista Trail across the valley floor.

2.1 At the junction with Cactus Wren Trail (GPS: 33.738795, -112.079395), keep right on Valle Vista Trail.

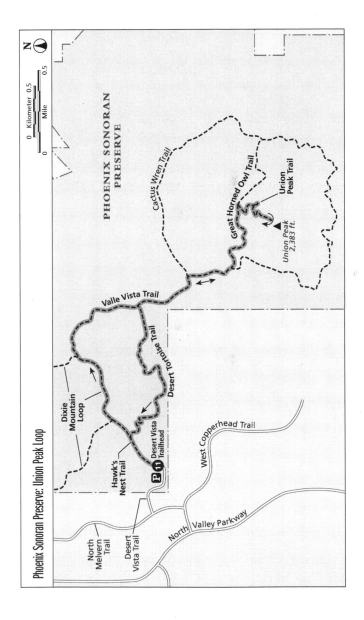

Phoenix Sonoran Preserve: Union Peak Loop

PHOENIX SONORAN PRESERVE

N

0 Kilometer 0.5
0 Mile 0.5

Cactus Wren Trail

Great Horned Owl Trail

Union Peak Trail

Union Peak 2,383 ft.

Valle Vista Trail

Desert Tortoise Trail

Dixie Mountain Loop

Hawk's Nest Trail

Desert Vista Trailhead

West Copperhead Trail

North Melvern Trail

Desert Vista Trail

North Valley Parkway

2.4 Reach the end of Valle Vista Trail at a three-way junction (GPS: 33.735265, -112.078547). Go left on Great Horned Owl Trail and hike on the northwest slope of Union Peak.

2.9 Reach the junction of Great Horned Owl Trail and Union Peak Trail (GPS: 33.734771, -112.072335). Go right on Union Peak Trail and climb 550 feet to the summit.

3.4 Arrive at the rocky summit of Union Peak (GPS: 33.731805, -112.074056). Return down the trail to a junction.

3.9 Reach the junction with Great Horned Owl Trail. Go left.

4.4 Reach a three-way junction. Go right on Valle Vista Trail.

5.2 Reach a junction with Desert Tortoise Trail. Go left and hike southwest on Desert Tortoise.

6.3 Reach a junction with Hawk's Nest Trail. Go left and return downhill on Hawk's Nest Trail to the trailhead.

6.6 Arrive back at the trailhead and parking lot (GPS: 33.741167, -112.097249).

12 Phoenix Sonoran Preserve: Apache Wash Trails Loop

This easy hike explores desert washes and saguaro-studded hillsides and offers spectacular views across the Sonoran Preserve in northern Phoenix.

Distance: 4.4 miles

Hiking time: 2–3 hours

Type of hike: Lollipop loop

Trail names: Ocotillo Trail, Apache Wash Trail, Sidewinder Trail, Ridgeback Trail, Ridgeback Overlook Trail

Difficulty: Moderate. Cumulative elevation gain is 559 feet.

Best season: Oct through Apr. Summers are hot with no shade.

Water availability: No potable water; restrooms at the trailhead

Restrictions: Parking and entrance open 5 a.m. to 7 p.m.; trails open 5 a.m. to 11 p.m.; park entrance gated after hours. Dogs must be leashed and waste promptly picked up; trails closed to dogs if temperatures exceed 100°F. No glass containers.

Maps: USGS New River SE; Phoenix Parks website

Trail contacts: Phoenix Parks and Recreation Department (see appendix); Ranger office: (602) 495-6939

Finding the trailhead: From I-17 north of Phoenix, take exit 222 to Dove Valley Road. Drive east on Dove Valley Road for 5.4 miles to a left turn to the Apache Wash Trailhead. This turn is just after Dove Valley Road becomes Sonoran Desert Drive. Drive a half mile to a large parking area and the Apache Wash Trailhead on the northeast side of the car park (GPS: 33.768058, -112.044539). Trailhead address: 1600 East Sonoran Dr.

The Hike

Spreading across more than 9,600 acres in the northern Phoenix area, the Sonoran Preserve includes two large tracts with intact Sonoran Desert ecosystems, providing habitat protection for plants and wildlife and offering human-powered recreation including almost 40 miles of hiking trails. Besides the Union Hills area (Hike 11), the Apache Wash sector is a marvelous place for a desert adventure.

This hike, beginning at the Apache Wash Trailhead, makes an easy loop on four trails with gentle grades, good foot surfaces, and expansive views of rocky hills, rugged slopes dotted with saguaros, and open plains along Apache Wash. All trail junctions are well marked with signposts. The trailhead area offers plenty of parking, restrooms, interpretive signs, and a shady ramada, but not drinking water.

A trailhead sign details the dangers of desert heat, a thermometer with the current temperature, and how much water to carry and drink for a two-hour hike in summer's sweltering weather. In the Danger range between 95°F and 105°F, carry at least five 16.9-ounce bottles of liquid. If temperatures are in the Extreme Danger range above 105°F, which is during most of the summer, carry at least seven bottles per person. Heat can kill, so hike wisely. Also, remember that dogs are not allowed on trails if temperatures exceed 100°F. No shade is found along the hike.

Miles and Directions

0.0 From the Apache Wash Trailhead, walk northeast on a sidewalk past trash cans, restrooms, a kiosk with maps and park info, and shade ramadas.

0.05 Reach a four-way junction after the sidewalk ends (GPS: 33.768666, -112.044006). Go left on Ocotillo Trail (O) and hike northwest.

0.3 Pass a trail junction to the left. Keep straight on Ocotillo Trail (O).

0.4 Reach a junction on the right with Apache Wash Trail (AW) (GPS: 33.771393, -112.048792) and the start of the loop. Go right on Apache Wash Trail and hike north. Ocotillo Trail goes left and is the return trail.

0.75 Reach a signed junction with two trails on the right by a large saguaro (GPS: 33.776125, -112.046879). Go left on Sidewinder Trail (S) and hike northwest. Sidewinder Trail is the first trail on the right and Apache Wash Trail (AW) is the second on the right.

1.2 Reach a junction on the right with a connector trail labeled "To Apache Wash Loop" (GPS: 33.781631, -112.050628). Keep left on Sidewinder Trail (S) and hike northwest on the southern slope of a broad ridge, passing a connector trail on the right that goes north to 14th Street and then steadily climbing.

2.0 Bend around the west side of the ridge and reach a junction on the left with Ridgeback Trail (R) (GPS: 33.782658, -112.059680). Go left on Ridgeback Trail and hike south past saguaros, clumps of teddy bear and buckhorn cholla cactus, ocotillos, and palo verde trees. This hike section offers solitude and fine views east to the McDowell Mountains and south to the humped Ridgeback Overlook.

2.9 After making several switchbacks, reach a junction with Ridgeback Overlook Trail on the north side of the mountain (GPS: 33.774317, -112.055304). Go right on signed Ridgeback Overlook Trail and hike south along a ridge crest.

3.0 Reach the rocky summit of 2,164-foot Ridgeback Overlook (GPS: 33.772999, -112.055506) and take a breather to enjoy scenic views east across Paradise Valley to Pinnacle Peak and the McDowells and the Phoenix Mountains,

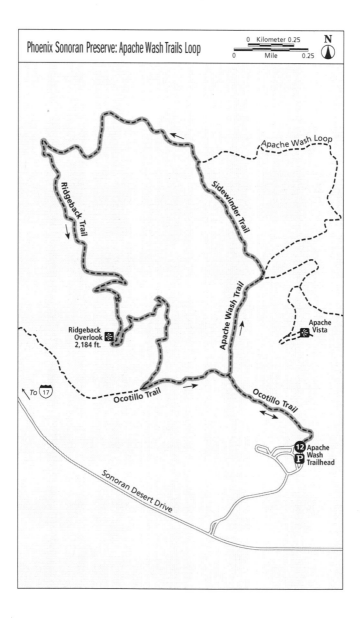

Phoenix Sonoran Preserve: Apache Wash Trails Loop

Kilometer 0.25

Mile 0.25

N

Apache Wash Loop

Sidewinder Trail

Ridgeback Trail

Apache Wash Trail

Ridgeback Overlook 2,184 ft.

Apache Vista

To 17

Ocotillo Trail

Ocotillo Trail

12 Apache Wash Trailhead P

Sonoran Desert Drive

including Piestewa Peak, to the south. Afterward, descend from the east side of the summit and hike north on Ridgeback Overlook Trail.

3.15 Arrive at a junction with Ridgeback Trail (R) (GPS: 33.774034, -112.054653) and go right on it. Descend the steep east slope of the mountain, following a blunt ridge and contouring across cactus-covered slopes to its southern base.

3.7 Reach a junction with Ocotillo Trail (O) below the mountain (GPS: 33.770692, -112.053889) and go left on Ocotillo Trail.

4.0 Return to a junction with Apache Wash Trail (AW) (GPS: 33.771382, -112.048854) and go right. Hike southeast on the wide trail to the first junction and go right on the sidewalk.

4.4 Arrive back at the trailhead (GPS: 33.768082, -112.044545).

13 Deem Hills Recreation Area: Palisade to Basalt to Circumference Trails

This loop hike, following three different trails, traverses a volcanic hill in the northeast corner of the park.

Distance: 1.6 miles
Hiking time: About 1 hour
Type of hike: Loop
Trail names: Water Tower Road, Palisade Trail, Basalt Trail, Circumference Trail
Difficulty: Moderate with easy grades on good surfaces; boulders on trail
Best season: Oct through Apr. Summers are hot.

Water availability: Water available at the trailhead
Restrictions: Trailhead and parking open 6 a.m. to 7 p.m. Trail open 5 a.m. to 11 p.m. Dogs must be leashed.
Maps: USGS Hedgepeth Hills; Phoenix Parks website
Trail contacts: Glendale Parks and Recreation (see appendix); Ranger office: (602) 495-6939

Finding the trailhead: The hike starts from the East Trailhead on North 39th Avenue. Access the trailhead and park from I-17 in north Phoenix. Take exit 218 for Happy Valley Road off I-17. Go left (west) on Happy Valley Road for a mile to North 35th Avenue and turn right (north) and drive 1.4 miles to Pinnacle Vista Road (35th Avenue bends right and turns into 33rd Avenue partway up). Turn left (west) on Pinnacle Vista Road and drive 0.7 mile until it dead-ends. Turn right on North 39th Avenue and drive 0.1 mile to the parking lot and trailhead on the left (GPS: 33.733476, -112.143611). East Trailhead address: 27428 N. 39th Ave.

The Hike

The Deem Hills, with almost 1,000 acres protected in Deem Hills Recreation Area, is a low range of volcanic hills that rises west of I-17 in north Glendale. Seven trails totaling 14 miles wind over the two main hills, including the unnamed 2,110-foot-high point, informally named "Wildcat Peak." The park, with two trailheads, is an undeveloped desert area that offers a great escape from the surrounding suburbs.

The described hike, following Palisade Trail up Water Tower Road to Basalt Trail and then descending Circumference Trail in the park's northeast quarter, has gentle grades on a paved and rocky trail surface. This easy hike is ideal for a family outing in springtime when colorful wildflowers blotch the barren hills. Brown posts at junctions mark the various trails with mileages and directions, making route finding a breeze.

The Deem Hills are covered with typical Arizona Upland vegetation, including saguaro cacti, barrel cacti, buckhorn cholla, hackberry and palo verde trees, creosote, and wildflowers, including brittlebush and globe mallow. The rocky hills are home to wildlife like coyotes, javelinas, and rattlesnakes. If you encounter a rattler on the trail, step back and let him escape into the rocks.

Begin your Deem Hills adventure at the East Trailhead off North 39th Street. Next to the parking lot is a map sign, shady ramada, and drinking fountain. Start by hiking north on the flat Circumference Trail for 0.05 mile or 275 feet to a junction with Water Tower Road and the second hike segment up Palisade Trail. Turn left on the closed paved road and hike west uphill.

The Palisade Trail ascends the rising road. Tall saguaros, palo verde trees, and yellow-flower brittlebush line the paved road. Turn left before the water tower onto Palisade Trail, a rock-lined dirt path.

The trail climbs south beneath a black-browed escarpment composed of black basalt boulders, which were formed by lava flows between 2 and 5 million years ago. Make a stop at the 0.5-mile post and check out irregular-shaped basalt blocks beside the trail. Note holes in the rock left by air bubbles when the lava quickly cooled.

Continue climbing, passing a couple stately saguaros with multiple arms, to the junction of Palisade and Basalt Trails. Go left on the Basalt Trail, the next 0.1-mile hike segment. The Palisade Trail heads up right, climbing onto a ridgetop to the south and then descending east.

The Basalt Trail goes east to a junction with the Circumference Trail. The last hike section follows the Circumference Trail down to the trailhead. Go left at the junction and descend the rocky trail, stepping over basalt boulders and passing scattered saguaros, some with cactus wren nests in holes. Volcanic rock from the Deem Hills was used by native peoples for thousands of years, fashioning the basalt into manos and metates for grinding corn and using white chalcedony for knives, arrow points, and scrapers. At the bottom of the hill, the trail crosses a bajada or outwash plain and reaches the end of another great desert hike.

Miles and Directions

0.0 Start at the East Trailhead on the north side of the parking area. Hike north on the Circumference Trail to a closed road.

0.05 Reach Water Tower Road (GPS: 33.734079, -112.143664). Go left up the paved road and gently climb west toward the

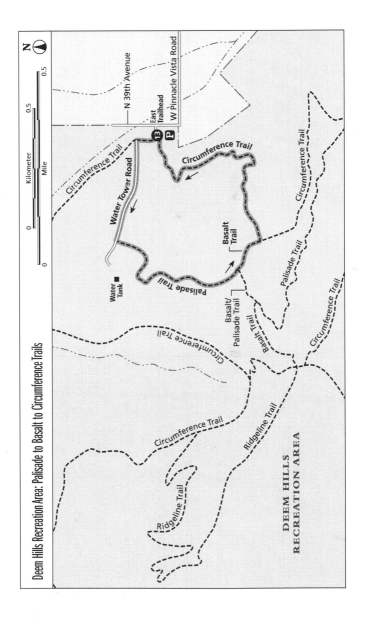

Deem Hills Recreation Area: Palisade to Basalt to Circumference Trails

water tower. The road is used by service vehicles so yield to traffic.

0.3 Reach the junction of the road and Palisade Trail (GPS: 33.734765, -112.147893). Go left on Palisade Trail and hike south past a rocky bluff.

0.8 Reach the junction of Palisade and Basalt Trails (GPS: 33.730643, -112.149049). Keep left on Basalt Trail.

0.9 Reach the junction of Basalt and Circumference Trails (GPS: 33.729910, -112.147900). Go left on the Circumference Trail, climbing to its broad summit and then descending northeast on rocky slopes.

1.6 Arrive back at the trailhead (GPS: 33.733476, -112.143611).

14 Thunderbird Conservation Park: Arrowhead Point Trail

This lollipop hike switchbacks to the scenic summit of Arrowhead Point in Thunderbird Conservation Area in north Glendale.

Distance: 2.6 miles
Hiking time: 2–3 hours
Type of hike: Lollipop
Trail names: Coach Whip Trail, Arrowhead Point Trail
Difficulty: Moderate with easy grades on good trail surfaces
Best season: Oct through Apr. Summers are hot.
Water availability: None
Restrictions: The trailhead is open from sunrise to sunset; the gate is locked at sunset. Dogs must be leashed and dog waste picked up. Dogs are not allowed on trails if temperatures exceed 100°F; violators are punished by fines and possible jail time.
Maps: USGS Hedgepeth Hills; park website
Trail contact: Glendale Parks and Recreation (see appendix)

Finding the trailhead: Access the trailhead and park from I-17 in north Phoenix. Take the Pinnacle Peak Road exit 217 and turn west on Pinnacle Peak Road. Drive west for 3.7 miles to 5413 West Pinnacle Peak Road and turn left or south into a large parking lot and the trailhead (GPS: 33.697417, -112.177953).

The Hike

Arrowhead Point Trail is a scenic hike that climbs to the summit of 1,862-foot Arrowhead Point, the second highest point in the Hedgepeth Hills in north Glendale. The hills, named for early settler Robert Hedgepeth, and the trail explore a desert range protected in 1,185-acre Thunderbird Conservation Park. The rugged hills in this desert preserve tuck into a suburban landscape of streets and subdivisions.

The park offers 14 miles of hiking on eight popular trails that range from a quarter mile to 5 miles long. Arrowhead Point Trail is one of the park's best hikes since it reaches a high summit with expansive views across north Phoenix and Glendale.

Begin at a trailhead at the southwest corner of a parking lot on the south side of Pinnacle Peak Road in the northeast quadrant of Thunderbird Conservation Park. A picnic table and signs detailing the park regulations and trails are at the trailhead.

The first hike section heads southwest on Coach Whip Trail (H1) across a flat valley. After a junction with Flatlander Trail (H1A), which goes left and loops around the valley, continue straight and climb a boulder-covered mountainside.

At another trail junction, go left or east on Arrowhead Point Trail (H2). The right trail is the return side of the loop hike. The wide trail, with gradual grades, switchbacks up the northern slopes of a humped mountain, threading through rounded basalt boulders from ancient lava flows. Higher are gentle slopes covered with yellow-flowered brittlebush, scrubby palo verde trees, and scattered saguaro cacti that rise like sentinels above the suburbs below.

After a viewpoint on a rocky knob, follow the boulder-lined trail to a spacious summit. A huge rock cairn or pile of rocks topped with a flapping American flag on a pole marks the summit of Arrowhead Point. The Deem Hills, conical Pyramid Peak, and Ludden Mountain rise to the north beyond the Hedgepeth Hills, while Arrowhead Lakes subdivision spreads to the south in Glendale.

After enjoying the view, head west on the trail, which descends along a broad ridge to a rocky overlook. Here the trail turns sharply east at a switchback and descends the broad northwest face of Arrowhead Point to a junction with Coach Whip Trail at the mountain base. Finish by following the Coach Whip/Arrowhead Trails back to the trailhead.

Miles and Directions

0.0 Start at the trailhead at the southwest corner of the parking lot. Hike southwest on Coach Whip Trail across a wide, flat valley.

0.15 Reach a junction with Flatlander Trail at the southwest edge of the valley (GPS: 33.695519, -112.178726). Continue straight on Arrowhead Point Trail and begin climbing the north flank of Arrowhead Point.

0.3 Reach a T-junction where Arrowhead Point Trail splits, forming a loop (GPS: 33.694450, -112.179212). Go left and follow the trail uphill. The right trail, also part of Coach Whip Trail, is the return trail.

0.8 Cross a sloping area below the summit.

1.0 The trail bends south and ascends a wide ridge.

1.2 Arrive at the summit of Arrowhead Point with its large rock cairn and flag (GPS: 33.689198, -112.179515). Enjoy the view, sip water, and munch a snack, then descend west on a ridge.

1.5 Reach the west end of the ridge. Go down right on the rocky trail across north-facing slopes.

2.0 Reach a junction with Coach Whip Trail at the mountain's base and a picnic ramada (GPS: 33.691860, -112.184399). Keep right on Coach Whip Trail past a pedestrian bridge on the left that crosses North 59th Avenue.

2.4 Reach the junction at the start of Arrowhead Point Trail loop. Go left and descend to the valley floor.

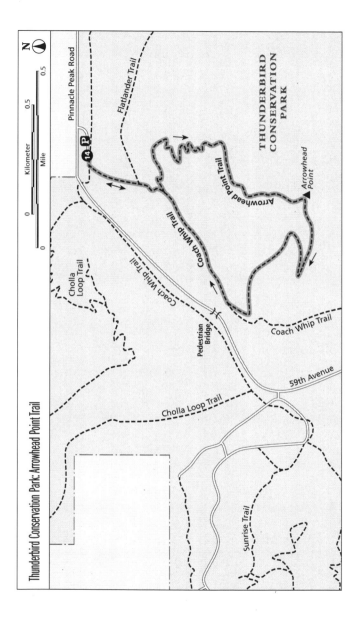

Thunderbird Conservation Park: Arrowhead Point Trail

N

Kilometer
0   0.5
0   0.5
Mile

Pinnacle Peak Road

14 P

Flatlander Trail

THUNDERBIRD
CONSERVATION
PARK

Arrowhead Point Trail

Arrowhead
Point

Coach Whip Trail

Coach Whip Trail

Coach Whip Trail

Pedestrian
Bridge

Cholla Loop Trail

59th Avenue

Cholla Loop Trail

Sunrise Trail

2.5 Reach the junction with Flatlander Trail. Continue straight on Coach Whip Trail across the valley.

2.6 Arrive back at the trailhead (GPS: 33.697417, -112.177953).

15 South Mountain Park: Dirt Road Trail–Pima Wash Trail

This easy hike follows a closed road and returns on a trail through a wide wash in South Mountain Park, the largest city park in the United States.

Distance: 2.8 miles
Hiking time: 1–2 hours
Type of hike: Loop
Trail names: Dirt Road Trail, Pima Wash Trail
Difficulty: Moderate. Elevation gain is 225 feet.
Best season: Nov through Apr
Water availability: Water available at the Pima Canyon Trailhead
Restrictions: Entrance and parking lot hours 5 a.m. to 7 p.m. June 1 to Sept 30 hours are 5 a.m. to 9 p.m. Trail hours are 5 a.m. to 11 p.m. Dogs must be leashed, and dog waste picked up. Dogs are not allowed on trails if temperatures exceed 100°F; violators are punished by fines and possible jail time. No glass containers. Do not leave the trail.
Maps: USGS Guadalupe topo map (trail not shown); park trail map; Phoenix Parks website
Trail contacts: Phoenix Parks and Recreation Department (see appendix); Ranger office: (602) 262-7393

Finding the trailhead: From I-10, take Baseline Road exit (155). Drive west on West Baseline Road for 0.6 mile to South 48th Street and turn left (south). Drive south on South 48th Street for 0.6 mile to a roundabout where the road continues as South Point Parkway. Continue south until the road rejoins South 48th Street (1.6 miles from Baseline). Turn right onto South 48th Street and left into Phoenix South Mountain Park. Follow East Pima Canyon Road until it ends at a parking lot and the Pima Canyon Trailhead (GPS: 33.362877, -111.985903). Street address: 4500 East Pima Canyon Rd.

The Hike

This 2.8-mile loop hike, following Dirt Road Trail up closed Pima Canyon Road and returning down Pima Wash Trail, is an easy and popular excursion in the eastern sector of South Mountain Park. The park, encompassing 16,283 acres of desert south of Phoenix, is the largest municipal park in the United States. A network of over 50 miles of multiuse trails explore the rugged range.

Your hiking adventure begins at the Pima Canyon Trailhead on the west end of the parking lot on the east side of South Mountain Park. Restrooms, drinking water, and three picnic ramadas are at the trailhead. On the mountain slope south of the parking lot is a fenced boulder with the inscription "Marcos de Niza" scratched into its surface. The Spanish explorer passed through in 1539, but the veracity of the inscription is debatable since no evidence indicates that de Niza did indeed carve it. A short trail scrambles to the boulder.

Dirt Road Trail heads west up broad Pima Canyon, flanking a deep wash. The canyon is arid, with scrubby creosote and bursage bushes scattered across rocky slopes. As the trail climbs, the vegetation changes. The rocky upper part of the canyon has more cacti, including saguaros, and palo verde trees. The road ends at a reclaimed parking lot and the ruins of two stone buildings—the remains of old picnic shelters. The National Trail hike begins here (see Hike 16).

The hike's return half starts at the road's end. Hike past a sign for the National Trail and drop into Pima Wash on Pima Wash Trail. The trail follows the deep wash back to the trailhead and parking lot, winding along the sandy floor or traversing open flats. The wash offers habitat for many bird species.

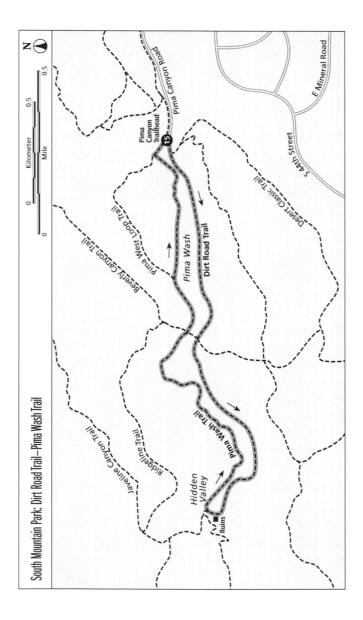

South Mountain Park: Dirt Road Trail–Pima Wash Trail

N

0   0.5   Kilometer
0   0.5   Mile

Pima Canyon Trailhead

Pima Canyon Road

15

Beverly Canyon Trail

Pima West Loop Trail

Pima Wash

Dirt Road Trail

Desert Classic Trail

S 44th Street

E Mineral Road

Pima Wash Trail

Hidden Valley

Ruins

Ridgeline Trail

Javelina Canyon Trail

Miles and Directions

0.0   Start at the Pima Canyon Trailhead on the west side of the parking lot (GPS: (GPS: 33.362877, -111.985903). Hike west on Dirt Road Trail (closed Pima Canyon Road).

1.3   Reach the road's end at the ruins of an old picnic area. Look for a sign for National Trail and go north on the rocky trail (GPS: 33.360862, -112.004978). Hike 150 feet to a junction with Pima Wash Trail.

1.35 At the junction of National Trail and Pima Wash Trail (GPS: 33.361226, -112.004888), go right on Pima Wash Trail and hike east down the wash.

2.2   Leave the wash and follow a bench above the wash's north bank.

2.7   Reach the end of Pima Wash Trail (GPS: 33.363655, -111.985994). Go right on a connector trail up the south bank of the wash to the parking lot.

2.8   Arrive back at a trailhead on the north side of the parking lot (GPS: 33.363106, -111.985117).

16 South Mountain Park: National–Mormon Loop Trails

This excellent loop hike offers spectacular scenery, spacious views, and interesting terrain, including a tunnel, Hidden Valley, and squeezing through Fat Man's Pass.

Distance: 6.4 miles
Hiking time: 3–4 hours
Type of hike: Loop
Trail names: Dirt Road Trail, National Trail, Hidden Valley Trail, Mormon Trail, Mormon Loop Trail
Difficulty: Moderately challenging. Elevation gain is 590 feet.
Best season: Nov through Apr
Water availability: Water available at the Pima Canyon Trailhead
Restrictions: Entrance and parking lot hours 5 a.m. to 7 p.m. June 1 to Sept 30 hours are 5 a.m. to 9 p.m. Trail hours are 5 a.m. to 11 p.m. Dogs must be leashed, and dog waste picked up. Dogs are not allowed on trails if temperatures exceed 100°F; violators are punished by fines and possible jail time. No glass containers. Do not leave the trail and shortcut.
Maps: USGS Guadalupe and Lone Butte topo maps (not up to date with trails); park trail map; Phoenix Parks website
Trail contacts: Phoenix Parks and Recreation Department (see appendix); Ranger office: (602) 262-7393

Finding the trailhead: From I-10, take Baseline Road exit (155). Drive west on West Baseline Road for 0.6 mile to South 48th Street and turn left (south). Drive south on South 48th Street for 0.6 mile to a roundabout where the road continues as South Point Parkway. Continue south until the road rejoins South 48th Street (1.6 miles from Baseline). Turn right onto South 48th Street and left into Phoenix South Mountain Park. Follow East Pima Canyon Road until it ends at a parking lot and the Pima Canyon Trailhead (GPS: 33.362877, -111.985903). Street address: 4500 East Pima Canyon Rd.

The Hike

South Mountain Park, a rugged mountain range bordering Phoenix, is one of the largest urban parks in the world. The vast parkland, a treasure for hikers, equestrians, and mountain bikers, is laced by over 50 miles of trails. The park also preserves desert wilderness and wildlife on the southern edge of America's fifth-largest city.

One of the park's best loop hikes, it follows the National Trail to Hidden Valley and then finishes down Mormon Loop Trail. This hike offers scenic views, unique geological formations, Native American rock art, and unusual plant life. Carry plenty of water and wear a hat, as little shade is found along the trail. Water is available at the trailhead. Watch for mountain bikers on the trails, although they are supposed to yield to hikers.

Start at the Pima Canyon Trailhead at the parking lot at the end of East Pima Canyon Road. The first hike segment follows Dirt Road Trail up closed Pima Canyon Road to the ruins of a couple stone picnic shelters.

The next section follows National Trail to the turnoff to Hidden Valley. The trail climbs a wide ridge, passing rock outcrops, ocotillos, and palo verde trees, and reaches the ridge crest after a couple miles. Farther west the trail twists into a shallow valley to a junction with Hidden Valley Trail.

This next half mile of trail threads through a marvelous scenic canyon to Hidden Valley—a concealed, isolated drainage high on South Mountain. Past Hidden Valley stretches a water-polished tunnel capped by an immense boulder. The sides of this cool passageway are slick from countless flash floods roaring down the canyon. Past the tunnel, ramble up a sandy wash to a 10-foot-high rock step and scramble up smooth boulders to exposed bedrock above.

The trail bends west and heads toward obvious boulders. Scan rocks south of the trail to see ancient Native American petroglyphs pecked into the varnished rock surface. The Hohokam and Pima peoples hunted game and gathered seeds on South Mountain. Archaeological sites here include rock art panels, grinding holes, and shrines. Scramble over water-polished slabs and through rounded boulders into another gravel wash flanked by ridges dotted with saguaro cacti, palo verdes, and brittlebushes. South Mountain is the northernmost locale for the elephant tree, a squat desert tree that typically grows in northern Mexico.

Follow the wash to a jumble of boulders and the famed Fat Man's Pass. This 25-foot-long passage between two large boulders is more of a fat man's nightmare, narrowing to a foot at its midsection. Kids delight in romping through the narrow corridor. If you don't want to squeeze through, scramble out of the wash before the boulders. Continue along the trail and rejoin National Trail. Go right on it and hike to the junction of National Trail and Mormon Loop Trail at an elevation of 1,960 feet. Go right on Mormon Loop Trail.

The trail descends east on a broad ridge to a pass with distant views across the Valley of the Sun and Phoenix. Continue across dry slopes covered with not-so-cuddly teddy bear cholla cacti to the bottom of a canyon. Look for petroglyph panels, including spirals and geometric designs, on rock outcroppings on the canyon's south side. Continue east to the starting point of the loop at the junction of Mormon Loop and National Trails.

Go right on National Trail to the old picnic area and hike east on Dirt Road Trail, the closed Pima Canyon Road, to the trailhead.

Miles and Directions

0.0   Begin at the Pima Canyon Trailhead at the west end of the parking lot. Hike west up closed Dirt Road Trail in a canyon.

1.3   Reach the end of Dirt Road Trail at the stone ruins of old picnic shelters. Look for a sign for the National Trail and go north on the rocky trail (GPS: 33.360862, -112.004978) and pass a junction on the right with Pima Wash Trail. Continue up a switchback on National Trail.

1.35 Reach the junction of National Trail and Mormon Loop Trail on the right (GPS: 33.361449, -112.005029). Keep left on National Trail and hike west up a long ridge with great views.

2.6   Reach the junction with Hidden Valley Trail on the left (GPS: 33.354827, -112.018424). Go left on Hidden Valley Trail and hike south to a tunnel through boulders. Continue southwest in a sandy wash through Hidden Valley, an open area surrounded by boulders and small cliffs.

3.1   Reach huge boulders blocking the wash and squeeze through Fat Man's Pass, a narrow corridor.

3.15 Reach a junction with National Trail and go right on it (GPS: 33.350926, -112.022653).

3.6   Twist through rocky hills and reach the junction of National Trail and Mormon Trail. Continue north on Mormon Trail for another 0.2 mile to the junction of Mormon Trail and Mormon Loop Trail.

3.8   Reach the junction of Mormon Trail and Mormon Loop Trail (GPS: 33.357509, -112.021830). Go right on Mormon Loop Trail and hike east on a wide ridge and pass a junction on the left with Devastator Trail.

South Mountain Park: National–Mormon Loop Trails

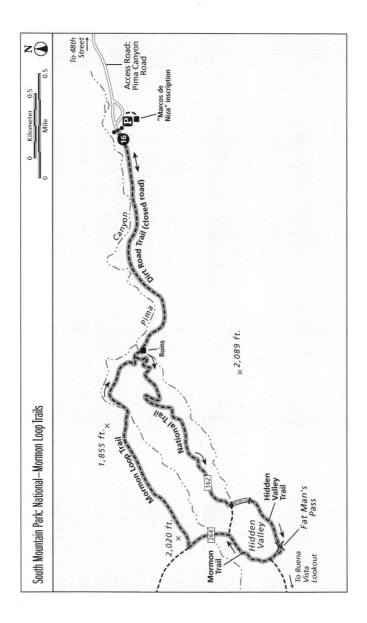

4.3 Reach a pass with views across South Mountain and Phoenix on a high ridge (GPS: 33.362383, -112.012379). Descend east into a canyon and pass a junction on the left with Javelina Trail (GPS: 33.363000, -112.006384). Keep right on Mormon Loop Trail.

5.1 Reach the first junction of Mormon Loop and National Trails. Go left on National Trail and descend past Pima Wash Trail to Dirt Road Trail.

6.15 Reach the junction with Dirt Road Trail at the old road's turn-around loop (GPS: 33.360759, -112.004912). Go right and follow Dirt Road Trail east above Pima Wash.

6.4 Arrive back at the trailhead (GPS: 33.362877, -111.985903).

17 Pinnacle Peak Park: Pinnacle Peak Trail

This excellent hike climbs up and around the granite summit block of Pinnacle Peak, a Phoenix-area landmark, and descends to a turn-around point west of the peak.

Distance: 3.95 miles

Hiking time: 2-3 hours

Type of hike: Out and back

Trail name: Pinnacle Peak Trail

Difficulty: Moderate to high point; strenuous for round trip. Elevation gain to high point is 295 feet; round trip is 900 feet.

Best season: Nov through Apr

Water availability: Water available at the trailhead

Restrictions: Open dawn to dusk daily; hours vary by the season. Closed on Christmas Day. No restrooms or water on the trail.

No dogs or bicycles; no smoking; no alcoholic beverages; no parking at the west side trail connection; no amplified music; no drones. Uphill hikers have the right of way. Yield to horses on the trail. Do not leave the designated trail; no off-trail hiking. A ranger station, restrooms, and water are at the trailhead.

Maps: USGS Currys Corner (trail not shown). Map on park website.

Trail contact: Pinnacle Peak Park (see appendix)

Finding the trailhead: Pinnacle Peak Park is in North Scottsdale, northeast of Phoenix. From the Pima Freeway (AZ 101), take exit 36 and drive north for 4.9 miles on Pima Road to Happy Valley Road. Turn right or east on Happy Valley and drive 1.9 miles to Alma School Road. Turn left or north on Alma School Road and drive 1 mile to Pinnacle Peak Parkway. Turn left on Pinnacle Peak Parkway, which becomes North 102nd Way, and drive 0.6 mile to a left turn to the parking lot and trailhead (GPS: 33.727642, -111.860745). Trailhead address: 26802 North 102nd Way, Scottsdale.

The Hike

Pinnacle Peak, a granite natural monolith perched atop a mountain pedestal, is one of the most distinctive landmarks in Phoenix and Scottsdale. The 3,169-foot peak, rising over 600 feet above the desert floor in northeast Scottsdale, is seen from miles away. Pinnacle Peak is the centerpiece of a 150-acre Scottsdale city park preserved as a natural area of cacti and wildlife. Despite being surrounded by the city's growing suburbs, the park offers a surprising amount of wildlife, including rattlesnakes, lizards, coyotes, foxes, and even occasional mountain lions on the prowl.

The park staff provides a variety of guided hikes, interpretive talks, full moon hikes, and astronomy talks in the winter months. Check the park website for a calendar of monthly activities and more about these programs.

The 1.95-mile Pinnacle Peak Trail traverses the park from east to west. This is not a loop hike. Many hikers go to the trail's high point, then return to the trailhead for a 1.3-mile trek. Most of the hiking is relatively easy on the hardpacked trail, with only a few steep, strenuous places. The western terminus of the trail ends at the park boundary, requiring hikers to return back to the trailhead.

The trail is rough in spots so wear good shoes, use sunscreen, and wear a hat. Carry at least a quart of water per person. Avoid lightning by keeping off high points on the trail in thunderstorms, especially in July and August. On busy days avoid conflict with other hikers by keeping to the right and not walking side by side on the narrow trail.

The hike begins at the trailhead beside the ranger station. The trail climbs steep switchbacks below Pinnacle Peak's precipitous summit block and then contours north across brushy slopes to the trail's high point north of the peak. This trail segment gains over 300 feet of elevation.

On the high ridge, stop and admire the vista from Grandview Point. To the south rises Pinnacle Peak, a granite pinnacle that formed over 1.4 billion years ago as molten rock slowly cooled into today's rock. The rounded natural monolith and the surrounding slabs and boulders were chiseled by millions of years of erosion using the persistent forces of water and weather.

From Grandview Point, the trail descends the west side of Pinnacle Peak and crosses rolling terrain studded with saguaros and cholla cacti, and interrupted by shallow washes lined with palo verde trees. At the park's western boundary, the hike ends just east of Jomax Road. Turn around here and return to the trailhead.

Miles and Directions

0.0 Start at the trailhead next to the park visitor center on the southwest side of the parking area. Hike west on the trail, switchbacking up east-facing slopes below Pinnacle Peak.

0.6 Reach Grandview Point, an overlook north of Pinnacle Peak (GPS: 33.730326, -111.865120). Continue south along a rocky ridge.

0.65 Reach an overlook and the trail's 2,889-foot high point (GPS: 33.729609, -111.864918). Hikers often turn around here, returning to the trailhead for a 1.3-mile hike. To continue, descend the trail on the west side of the ridge below Pinnacle Peak.

0.85 Reach Owl's Rest, an overlook enclosed by a circular stone wall. After admiring views across north Scottsdale and Phoenix, descend switchbacks on a steep rocky slope.

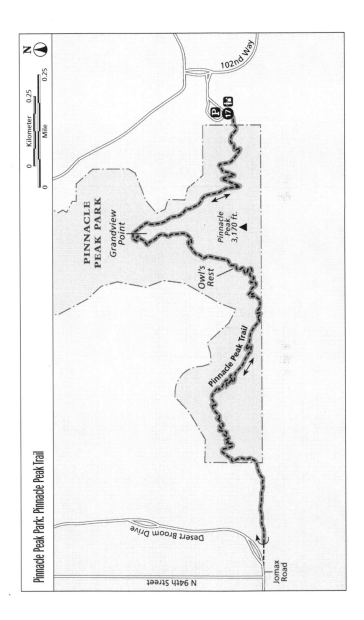

Pinnacle Peak Park: Pinnacle Peak Trail

1.95 Arrive at the end of the trail at 2,367 feet and the hike's turn-around point on the park's west boundary (GPS: 33.726708, -111.876851). Savor a gulp of water and hike back up the trail to Grandview Point and then descend the east side of Pinnacle Peak.

3.95 Arrive back at the trailhead (GPS: 33.727642, -111.860745).

18 McDowell Sonoran Preserve: Tom's Thumb, Feldspar, and Marcus Landslide Loop

This easy loop hike explores the northern edge of the scenic McDowell Mountains northeast of Scottsdale and Phoenix.

Distance: 1.5 miles
Hiking time: About 1 hour
Type of hike: Loop
Trail names: Tom's Thumb Trail, Feldspar Trail, Marcus Landslide Trail
Difficulty: Easy with minimal elevation on a good surface
Best season: Oct through Apr. Summers are hot.
Water availability: No water available at the trailhead; limited shade on trails
Restrictions: Trailhead open sunrise to sunset; gates open 30 minutes before sunrise and close at sunset. Dogs must be on a leash no longer than 6 feet; pick up dog waste immediately and dispose of it in a trash container; do not leave bagged dog waste by trails. It's recommended to leave dogs at home if temperatures exceed 90°F.
Maps: USGS McDowell Peak; McDowell Sonoran Preserve website
Trail contact: City of Scottsdale (see appendix)

Finding the trailhead: From AZ 101 (Pima Freeway), take exit 36 onto Pima Road and drive 4.9 miles north to Happy Valley Road. Turn right or east on Happy Valley Road and follow for 4.3 miles to Ranch Gate Road after it bends north and turns into 118th Street. Make a right or east turn on Ranch Gate Road (signed for preserve) and drive east for 1.3 miles to North 128th Street. Turn right on North 128th Street and drive 1.5 miles to two parking lots (GPS: 33.694461,

-111.801759) and the Tom's Thumb Trailhead. Trailhead address: 23015 North 128th St., Scottsdale.

The Hike

The McDowell Sonoran Preserve, with 30,580 acres protected by the City of Scottsdale, includes the McDowell Mountains and surrounding desert ecosystems. The area is open for nonmotorized recreation, including hiking, rock climbing, and nature study. The preserve, the largest city parkland in the United States, has four trailheads that offer over 180 miles of trail in its desert wildlands.

This excellent loop hike, following three trails—Tom's Thumb, Feldspar, and Marcus Landslide Trails—begins at the Tom's Thumb Trailhead at the park's northern end and explores a sloping outwash plain beneath a rugged canyon. The wide trails are easy to follow with a compact surface and minimal elevation gain. Signs with mileages mark all junctions so there's no way to get lost.

The hike is particularly good in March and April when wildflowers carpet the desert floor. No water is available at the trailhead, so bring plenty to hydrate along with sports drinks. And don't forget sunscreen, bug spray, and a hat.

Dogs are also welcome to hike on the preserve's trails but must be always leashed, and you must pick up all dog waste immediately and properly dispose of it. Remember to bring water for your pet. Dogs can easily overheat and die on hot desert days.

While the easily accessed hike is popular, lots of wildlife can be spotted by keen eyes and binoculars including eagles, hawks, desert tortoises, coyotes, and rattlesnakes. Pay attention when hiking on warm days since rattlers often sprawl across the trail to catch warming rays. Give them a wide berth and don't harm them—this is their desert home and you're the visitor.

Begin the hike on the south side of the east parking loop. Walk south to a large pavilion which offers cool shade on hot days along with restrooms and interpretative signs. Exit the south side of the pavilion onto Tom's Thumb Trail, a rugged trail that climbs 2.2 miles up a valley and steep slopes to prominent 3,970-foot-high Tom's Thumb, a fat granite appendage perched atop a high ridge directly south.

Follow the rolling trail south over gravel hillocks dotted with cholla cacti, prickly pear cacti, turpentine bushes, and mesquite and palo verde trees to a Y-junction with Mesquite Trail. Keep right on Tom's Thumb Trail. The wide path gently climbs toward the edge of the McDowell Mountains and reaches a junction with Feldspar Trail. Go left on Feldspar.

The next trail segment follows Feldspar Trail northeast along the edge of the mountains to Marcus Landslide Trail. The trail rises to its high point and then descends across dry washes to the junction with the Morrell's Wall climber access route. The McDowell Mountains, with its granite outcrops and cliffs, is a popular venue for Phoenix rock climbers.

After intersecting the Mesquite Trail again, keep straight on Feldspar Trail and walk past a giant boulder on the right and canyon with a dry streambed south of the trail. At a boulder pile the trail bends and skirts the mountain edge along a sandy wash and reaches the last junction with Marcus Landslide Trail. Go left on this trail.

Marcus Landslide Trail is a fine extra-credit hike. The 3-mile out-and-back hike, beginning at the parking lot, ends at the second largest landslide in Arizona. This interpretative geology hike passes cool rock formations, colorful spring

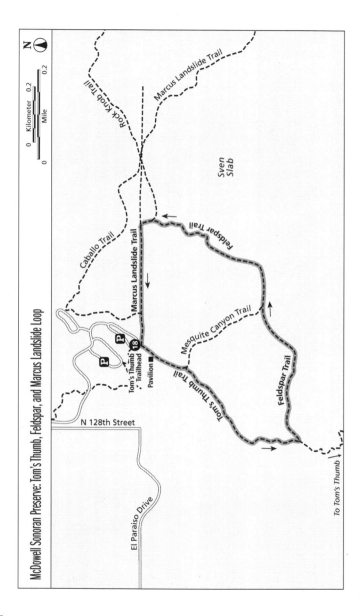

McDowell Sonoran Preserve: Tom's Thumb, Feldspar, and Marcus Landslide Loop

N

0   Kilometer   0.2
0   Mile   0.2

Rock Knob Trail

Marcus Landslide Trail

Caballo Trail

Marcus Landslide Trail

Sven Slab

Feldspar Trail

Mesquite Canyon Trail

Tom's Thumb Trail

Feldspar Trail

Tom's Thumb Trailhead

Pavilion

18

P

P

N 128th Street

El Paraiso Drive

To Tom's Thumb

wildflowers, and offers distant views east toward the Four Peaks.

The last segment follows Marcus Landslide Trail west through dry washes back to the parking lot's south side and the end of another stellar Phoenix hike.

Miles and Directions

0.0 Start from the Tom's Thumb Trailhead on the south side of the east parking lot (GPS: 33.694461, -111.801759). Walk through a ramada and follow marked Tom's Thumb Trail southwest.

0.1 Reach a junction with Mesquite Trail on the left (GPS: 33.692939, -111.802540). Continue straight on Tom's Thumb Trail up a wide bajada.

0.5 Meet the junction of Tom's Thumb Trail and Feldspar Trail (GPS: 33.689246, -111.805363). Go left on Feldspar Trail and hike along the mountain base.

0.7 Pass a climber access trail to Morrell's Wall. Continue northwest on a gravel ridge between washes.

0.9 Reach the junction of Feldspar and Mesquite Trails (GPS: 33.690488, -111.800195). Go straight on Feldspar Trail.

1.0 Pass a climber's trail on the right to Girlie Man, Sven Tower, and Hog Heaven.

1.2 Reach the junction with Marcus Landslide Trail (GPS: 33.693986, -111.796853). Go left or west on Marcus Landslide Trail.

1.5 Arrive back at the trailhead on the south side of the east parking lot (GPS: 33.694502, -111.801521).

19 McDowell Sonoran Preserve: Horseshoe Loop Hike

This scenic hike makes an easy loop across a cactus-studded outwash plain at the western side of the McDowell Mountains.

Distance: 1.7 miles
Hiking time: About 1 hour
Type of hike: Loop
Trail names: Saguaro Trail, Gateway Loop Trail, Horseshoe Trail, Desert Park Trail
Difficulty: Easy. Elevation gain is 100 feet on a good but rocky trail surface.
Best season: Oct through Apr. Summers are hot.
Water availability: Water available at the pavilion at the trailhead
Restrictions: Trailhead open sunrise to sunset; gates open 30 minutes before sunrise and close at sunset. Dogs must be on a leash no longer than 6 feet; pick up dog waste immediately and dispose of it in a trash container; do not leave bagged dog waste by trails. It's recommended to leave dogs at home if temperatures exceed 90°F.
Maps: USGS McDowell Peak; McDowell Sonoran Preserve website
Trail contact: City of Scottsdale (see appendix)

Finding the trailhead: From AZ 101 (Pima Freeway), take exit 36 onto Pima Road and drive north for 0.6 mile to the first major intersection and turn right or east on Union Hills Drive. Drive east on Union Hills for 1.2 miles until it dead ends at Thompson Peak Parkway. Turn right or south on the parkway and drive south for 1.1 miles to a left or east turn onto McDowells Foothills Drive, signed for the preserve. Follow it for 0.2 mile to several parking lots and the Gateway Trailhead on the right (GPS: 33.649438, -111.859007). Address: 18333 N. Thompson Peak Rd., Scottsdale.

Alternatively, exit AZ 101 at the Bell Road exit (either exit 39 from the south or exit 36 from the north) and drive to Bell Road. Turn east on Bell Road and drive 1.7 miles to Thompson Peak Parkway and turn left or north. Drive 0.7 mile to the Gateway Trailhead on the right.

The Hike

The McDowell Sonoran Preserve is a vast 30,580-acre natural reserve managed by the City of Scottsdale to protect the McDowell Mountains, which form the city's northeast skyline. The area offers over 180 miles of trails that explore rugged mountains, deep canyons and valleys, and broad bajadas or outwash plains studded with gardens of cacti and wildflowers. The trails at the Gateway Trailhead, including this hike, are well marked with signposts. Note that each is labeled with a marker number so you can be easily found in an emergency.

The easiest access to the preserve is the Gateway Trailhead area on the west side of the mountains with plenty of parking, a covered pavilion with restrooms, water, and interpretive displays including a 3D terrain map of the McDowells, and an outdoor amphitheater for educational programs. The Gateway has a zero annual carbon footprint; solar panels; rainfall collected from a roof catchment system and stored in an underground cistern. The building is composed of 30 percent recycled material and 47 percent regionally produced materials. More than 1,500 cacti were revegetated at the Gateway.

Begin the hike at the trailhead on the east side of the parking area at a paved trail. Walk east through the ramada and continue along an elevated walkway to the dirt surface of Saguaro Trail. After 0.1 mile reach the junction with the Bajada Nature Trail, a short accessible loop for families, seniors, and wheelchair trekkers who can experience the Sonoran Desert through interactive displays about plants, animals, seasons, cacti, trees, and pack rats. A left turn at this junction goes to the amphitheater. Continue straight on Saguaro Trail.

The next trail segment wanders across a sloping bajada below the ragged mountains. Saguaros, preferring the well-drained soils on bajadas, grow beside the trail and include cigar-shaped young ones to towering hundred-year-old specimens with multiple arms. Look also for fishhook barrel cacti, different species of cholla, creosote, and palo verde trees.

Saguaro Trail ends at a major junction with Gateway Loop Trail. Go left on it. For extra credit, take the short 0.3-mile Saguaro Loop Trail, which goes straight from the junction and makes a lollipop loop through a forest of saguaros.

The stony trail heads north, dipping across shallow washes and passing a dense group of teddy bear cholla. Don't let these spiny cacti mislead you—they're hardly cuddly! The joints break off if you stray too close to them with the long spines painfully grabbing your skin.

At the next junction, go left on Horseshoe Trail and cross a wide wash that drains southwest down a deep valley from the McDowells. Stop at the bottom of the wash and take in a great view of Tom's Thumb, the prominent squat pinnacle on a high ridge to the northeast. After leaving the wash, the trail crosses a gently sloping plain, passing more saguaros and teddy bear cholla gardens.

At the junction with Desert Park Trail, go left and hike south across level terrain passing tall mature saguaros and vistas east to the McDowell Mountains. End at the pavilion east of the trailhead and parking lots.

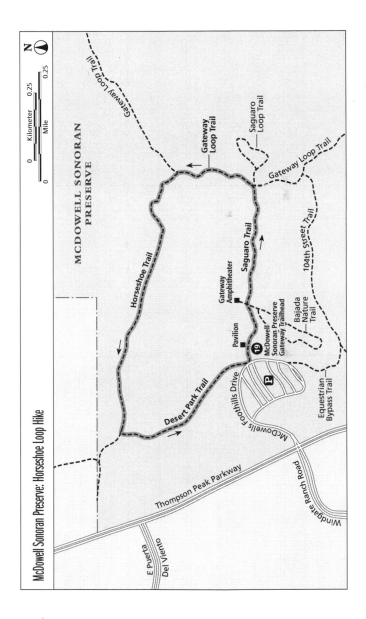

McDowell Sonoran Preserve: Horseshoe Loop Hike

Miles and Directions

0.0 Start at the Gateway Trailhead on a paved sidewalk (GPS: 33.649438, -111.859007). Walk east through the building on the paved trail and cross a steel walkway to the dirt Saguaro Trail.

0.1 Reach a junction on the right with Bajada Nature Trail (GPS: 33.649494, -111.856838). Go straight on Saguaro Trail.

0.4 Reach a junction with Gateway Loop Trail (GPS: 33.649310, -111.852107). Go left and hike north on it. The 0.3-mile Saguaro Loop Trail is a loop east of the junction.

0.6 Reach a Y-junction with Horseshoe Trail (GPS: 33.651889, -111.851536). Go left on it and hike west through washes and across stony plains.

1.3 Reach a junction with Desert Park Trail on the left (GPS: 33.653660, -111.861871). Go left and hike south past tall saguaros.

1.7 Arrive at the hike's end at the paved walkway between the Gateway Trailhead and the pavilion (GPS: 33.649493, -111.858939).

20 Usery Mountain Regional Park: Wind Cave Trail

This wonderful hike twists up the west side of 3,127-foot Pass Mountain South Peak to a shelter cave that offers scenic views.

Distance: 3.2 miles
Hiking time: 2-3 hours
Type of hike: Out and back
Trail names: Wind Cave Trail
Difficulty: Moderately challenging. Elevation gain is 812 feet.
Best season: Nov through Apr
Water availability: Water available at the trailhead
Restrictions: Park hours from May to Oct 5 a.m. to 9 p.m.; Nov 1 to Apr 30 6 a.m. to 8 p.m. Hiker-only trail. Leashed dogs only; properly remove and dispose of dog waste. To avoid damaging fragile desert ecosystems, do not leave the trail. No glass bottles, littering, fires, or camping.
Maps: USGS Apache Junction (trail not shown); Usery Mountain Recreation Area map; park website
Trail contacts: Usery Mountain Regional Park; Maricopa County Parks and Recreation Office; Tonto National Forest (see appendix)

Finding the trailhead: Drive east from Phoenix on US 60, the Superstition Freeway, to Ellsworth Road/East University Drive at exit 27. Exit onto East University and go east for a couple hundred feet. Turn left (north) on Ellsworth Road and drive 6.6 miles to Usery Mountain Regional Park's main entrance. Ellsworth Road turns into Usery Pass Road at the park's southern boundary. Turn right (east) into the park on Usery Park Road and drive past the visitor center on the right to the park entrance booth. Pay the daily entry fee and follow Usery Park Road to Wind Cave Drive. Turn left (north) on this one-way road and park at the lot at the north end of the loop (GPS: 33.474114, -111.607241).

The Hike

Usery Mountain Regional Park, a 3,324-acre Maricopa County Park northeast of Mesa, encompasses a desert area on the west flank of Pass Mountain. The mountain and the adjoining land east of the park are in Tonto National Forest. Although Wind Cave Trail, the most popular hike in the park, begins in the park, most of the trail is in the national forest.

The 1.5-mile trail climbs the abrupt western face of Pass Mountain to a large, scooped-out shelter cave in the volcanic tuff cliffs. This excellent hike offers marvelous views and a diverse Sonoran Desert ecosystem along a good trail with gentle grades.

Usery Mountain and the park are named for King Usery, a rancher, stagecoach robber, and rustler who lived here in the 1880s and 1890s. Usery held up a stage with Bill Blevins in 1891 for two silver bars. He was later captured at his ranch and sentenced to seven years in prison but was pardoned after two years.

The Wind Cave Trail, a hiker-only path, begins at the Wind Cave Trailhead on the north side of the parking area on Wind Cave Drive. Restrooms and water are here. Look for the trailhead sign right of the restroom. Be sure to carry plenty of water, especially if it's hot.

The hike heads north from the parking area and enters Tonto National Forest at a fence. Hike northeast up a sloping bajada, or outwash plain, below the towering west face of 3,312-foot Pass Mountain. The trail follows the edge of a wash filled with palo verde trees and rounded boulders.

Saguaro cacti, fishhook barrel cacti, chain cholla cacti, oco-tillos, and jojobas line the trail. In springtime, yellow brittle-bush flowers spread a colorful carpet across the desert. White bursage, a low shrub and the most common plant here, has a small, colorless flower because it is wind-pollinated and doesn't rely on attracting insects.

Reach a rest area after a half mile. Find the shade of a palo verde tree and a convenient boulder to sit on, catch your breath, and study the area's geologic formations. From the parking lot, the trail runs across 1.5-billion-year-old granite bedrock. The coarse granite also forms the lower slopes of Pass Mountain. Above the granite are obvious bands of Ter-tiary Age volcanic rocks. The lowest band is a tuff, or volcanic ash deposit, that forms prominent green cliffs striping the mountain's steep west face.

This deposit represents explosive volcanic eruptions that piled thick layers of ash atop the granite. Wind Cave, where the hike ends, is a long arching cave on the far right side of the tuff cliff. Above the tuff are long bands of dark basalt deposited as ancient lava flows on the west slope of South Pass Mountain.

Beyond here the trail steepens and climbs mountain slopes on gentle switchbacks. After reaching the tuff cliffs, turn south and contour along boulder-strewn slopes below the cliffs. The trail gradually rises to Wind Cave, an over-hanging alcove cave tucked under an 80-foot cliff.

This shady cave makes a cool spot to enjoy wide views. Straight west is the pyramidal Camelback Mountain ris-ing above Scottsdale. To its right is Piestewa Peak, another Phoenix landmark. The McDowell Mountains punctuate the northwest skyline. Closer at hand are the Usery Mountains,

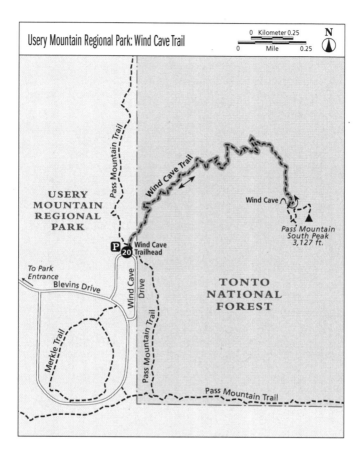

with "Phoenix" spelled in large white letters, and housing subdivisions in eastern Mesa.

Inside the cave are holes and water seeps. Wild geraniums dot the cave roof, creating a lush, hanging garden in springtime. Watch for bees and beehives in the cave; they, along with ground squirrels, take advantage of this oasis of water and shade.

If you have the energy and sufficient water, scramble to the 3,127-foot summit Pass Mountain South Peak. A 0.4-mile trail begins on the right side of the cave and angles up through cliff bands to the north ridge. The rocky trail threads through a cliff band and over boulders on the ridge. Spectacular views of the Goldfield and Superstition Mountains to the east are the rewards for standing on the airy summit.

Miles and Directions

0.0 Begin at the Wind Cave Trailhead on Wind Cave Drive. Hike north, passing a junction with Pass Mountain Trail, and continue northeast.

0.1 Reach the Tonto National Forest boundary fence. Continue northeast on Wind Cave Trail beside a deep arroyo.

0.5 Stop at a rest area and sip water. Continue hiking up steep slopes on the switchbacking trail.

1.1 Reach the base of a long cliff band formed of volcanic tuff. Follow the cliff base south.

1.6 Reach shady Wind Cave and the hike's turn-around point (GPS: 33.476702, -111.596851). After cooling down, return down the trail.

3.2 Arrive back at the trailhead (GPS: 33.474114, -111.607241).

21 Usery Mountain Regional Park: Merkle Trail

This easy hike loops around Headquarters Hill, exploring the unique Sonoran Desert ecosystem.

Distance: 0.95 mile
Hiking time: About 1 hour
Type of hike: Lollipop loop
Trail name: Merkle Trail
Difficulty: Easy. Elevation gain is 59 feet.
Best season: Nov through Apr
Water availability: Water and restrooms available at the trailhead
Restrictions: Park hours from May to Oct 5 a.m. to 9 p.m.; Nov 1 to Apr 30 6 a.m. to 8 p.m. Hiker-only trail. Leashed dogs only; properly remove and dispose of dog waste. To avoid damaging fragile desert ecosystems, do not leave the trail. No glass bottles, littering, fires, or camping.
Maps: USGS Apache Junction topo map (trail not shown); Usery Mountain Recreation Area map; park website
Trail contacts: Usery Mountain Regional Park; Maricopa County Parks and Recreation Office (see appendix)

Finding the trailhead: Drive east from Phoenix on US 60, the Superstition Freeway, to Ellsworth Road/East University Drive at exit 27. Exit here onto East University and go east for a couple hundred feet. Turn left (north) on Ellsworth Road and drive 6.6 miles to Usery Mountain Park's main entrance. Ellsworth Road turns into Usery Pass Road at the park's southern boundary. Turn right (east) into the park on Usery Park Road and drive past the visitor center on the right to the park entrance booth. Pay the daily fee and follow Usery Park Road, which turns into Blevins Drive, to a picnic area and parking lot on the right side of the road past Wind Cave Drive. The Merkle Trailhead is on the right side of the parking lot (GPS: 33.471207,

-111.608093). Alternatively, begin the trail at the south end of Blevins Drive at a parking lot and picnic area with ramadas (GPS: 33.466187, -111.611008).

The Hike

The Merkle Trail offers an easy loop hike around 2,078-foot Headquarters Hill, a low granite hill southwest of rugged Pass Mountain. The accessible trail is barrier-free for wheelchairs. Three picnic areas with shaded tables scatter along Blevins Drive, which parallels the trail, making this a fine hike to combine with a picnic lunch. Interpretive plaques along the trail identify desert plants you see along the trail. This is a hiker-only trail; horses and mountain bikes are not allowed. While the hike is described as starting from the picnic area on the north side of the hill, you can also begin at a parking lot south of the hill.

The hike begins at a trailhead on the right side of the parking lot north of Headquarters Hill on Blevins Drive. The wide trail heads south to a sandy wash and an obvious three-way junction. Take Merkle Trail's left fork. The right fork is the return trail and the trail going straight is 0.5-mile Vista Trail.

The trail contours along the base of Headquarters Hill above a broad wash lined with palo verde and ironwood trees. An east-facing bench lets you take in a spectacular view east to the rocky ramparts of the Superstition Mountains. The Superstitions are the site of the fabled Lost Dutchman Mine, a supposedly rich gold mine, the location of which was lost with the death of its owner Jacob Walz in 1892. Interpretive signs along the trail identify desert plants, including brittlebush, bursage, palo verde, mistletoe, ocotillo, and creosote bush.

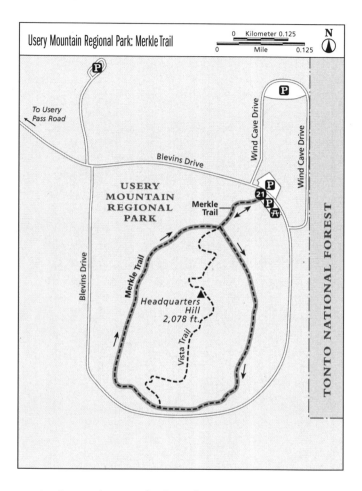

Usery Mountain Regional Park: Merkle Trail

0   Kilometer 0.125
0   Mile   0.125

N

To Usery
Pass Road

Blevins Drive

Wind Cave Drive

Wind Cave Drive

USERY
MOUNTAIN
REGIONAL
PARK

Merkle
Trail

21

Blevins Drive

Merkle Trail

Headquarters
Hill
2,078 ft.

Vista Trail

TONTO NATIONAL FOREST

At the southern end of Headquarters Hill are restrooms, a parking lot, and an alternative trailhead. Continue on the trail, bending north along the hill's western flank. Knobby granite boulders cover the hillside and saguaro cacti stand guard above like silent sentinels. This delightful trail section features lots of cacti, including hedgehog, pincushion, and fishhook barrel cacti. Look for young saguaros growing in the shade of palo verde nurse trees along the path. Reach the first junction at the north end of the hill. Finish by hiking left back to the trailhead and parking lot.

If you have the energy, the 0.5-mile Vista Trail, which goes right at the last junction, makes a fine extra-credit hike to the top of Headquarters Hill. The trail climbs to the top and then drops south to the park road.

Miles and Directions

0.0 Begin at the Merkle Trailhead on the right side of Blevins Drive. Hike past picnic ramadas and cross a dry wash.

0.09 Reach a three-way trail junction and go left on Merkle Trail (GPS: 33.470437, -111.609183) and hike south on the east side of the hill. The right trail is the return trail and straight is Vista Trail.

0.4 Reach the south end of Headquarters Hill and an alternative trailhead (GPS: 33.466187, -111.611008). Across the road are restrooms and parking. Continue straight on the main trail.

0.9 Reach the first junction with Vista Trail at the north end of the hill. Go left (north) on the main trail.

0.95 Arrive back at the trailhead (GPS: 33.471207, -111.608093).

22 McDowell Mountain Regional Park: Wagner and Granite Trails Loop

This fine easy hike for kids, families, and seniors circumnavigates the E. I. Rowland Campground.

Distance: 2.2 miles
Hiking time: About 1 hour
Type of hike: Loop
Trail names: Wagner Trail, Granite Trail, Spur Trail
Difficulty: Easy. Elevation gain is 125 feet.
Best season: Nov through Apr
Water availability: Water available at the campground trailhead
Restrictions: Park hours from May 1 to Oct 31 5 a.m. to 9 p.m.; Nov 1 to Apr 30 6 a.m. to 8 p.m. Hikers only. Leashed dogs only; properly remove and dispose of dog waste.
Maps: USGS Fort McDowell topo map (trail not shown); McDowell Mountain Regional Park trail map; park website
Trail contacts: McDowell Mountain Regional Park; Maricopa County Parks and Recreation Office (see appendix)

Finding the trailhead: From I-10, exit east to Loop 202. Follow Loop 202 to AZ 87 (Beeline Highway). Go north on AZ 87 to Shea Boulevard. Go left on Shea Boulevard and drive to Fountain Hills Boulevard. Continue north until the road turns into McDowell Mountain Road. Continue north to McDowell Mountain Park Drive and turn left into the park. From the park entrance, drive 2.7 miles to a turn onto Thoms Thumb Drive and E. I. Rowland Campground. Turn left and drive 0.1 mile to a hiker parking area and the Wagner Trailhead on the road's right side (GPS: 33.694216, -111.730996).

The Hike

This mostly level hike makes a circle around 21,099-acre McDowell Mountain Regional Park's E. I. Rowland Campground's north loop. The wide trails, with gentle grades, is a perfect hike for children or seniors.

The hike begins at the Wagner Trailhead on the north side of a parking lot on Thoms Thumb Drive, which heads west to the campground. The signed trailhead has a shaded kiosk with park information and maps, and a picnic table shaded by a palo verde tree. Follow Wagner Trail north and then bend west with the campground to your left.

The trail and county park, along with over 20,000 surrounding acres north and east of the McDowell Mountains, was charred by a raging brush fire started by lightning in the summer of 1995. Look for evidence of the devastation and the rejuvenation of the desert ecosystem along the trail, including weathered skeletons of dead saguaros. In springtime, enjoy a carpet of colorful wildflowers spreading across the desert floor.

The wide path heads west and crosses a spur road that ends at a park maintenance facility to the right. Past the road is a junction with Granite Trail. Go left on it and walk south. The trail meanders along the east side of a broad wash cut into a sloping outwash plain. Keep left at the next junction with Bluff Trail on the right and follow Granite Trail southeast to a Y-junction. Go left on Spur Trail until it ends at Rock Nob Road and go right on the road to Thoms Thumb Drive to return to the parking lot.

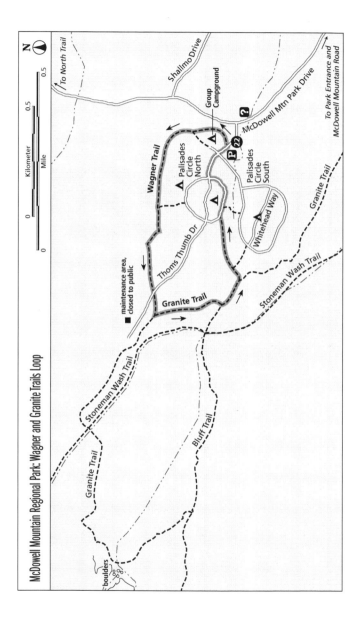

McDowell Mountain Regional Park: Wagner and Granite Trails Loop

N

Kilometer
0   0.5
Mile
0   0.5

To North Trail

Shallmo Drive

Group Campground

McDowell Mtn Park Drive

To Park Entrance and
McDowell Mountain Road

Wagner Trail

Palisades Circle North

Palisades Circle South

Whitehead Way

P
22
?

maintenance area, closed to public

Thoms Thumb Dr

Granite Trail

Stoneman Wash Trail

Granite Trail

Stoneman Wash Trail

Bluff Trail

boulders

Miles and Directions

0.0   Start at the Wagner Trailhead on the right side of Thoms Thumb Drive west of McDowell Mountain Park Drive and the park visitor center. Hike north and then west on signed Wagner Trail north of the campground.

1.0   Reach a park maintenance road. Cross at a crosswalk and continue west on Wagner Trail.

1.1   Reach a T-junction with Granite Trail (GPS: 33.698623, -111.743364). Go left on Granite Trail.

1.4   Three-way junction with Bluff Trail (GPS: 33.694508, -111.742586). Keep left on Granite Trail and hike south.

1.5   Reach a Y-junction with Spur Trail on the left (GPS: 33.693517, -111.740811). Go left on it and hike east toward the campground.

1.8   Reach Rock Nob Road in the campground opposite campsite #21 (GPS: 33.694655, -111.736224). Go right and follow Rock Nob Road and Thoms Thumb Drive through the campground to the trailhead.

2.2   Arrive back at the trailhead (GPS: 33.694216, -111.730996).

23 McDowell Mountain Regional Park: Wagner-Granite-Bluff Trails Loop

This easy hike, following four trails, loops through an arid Sonoran Desert landscape and offers spacious mountain views, solitude, and wildlife.

Distance: 4.8 miles

Hiking time: 2–3 hours

Type of hike: Loop

Trail names: Wagner Trail, Granite Trail, Bluff Trail, Spur Trail

Difficulty: Moderate. Cumulative elevation gain is 323 feet.

Best season: Nov through Apr

Water availability: Water available at the campground trailhead

Restrictions: Park hours from May 1 to Oct 31 5 a.m. to 9 p.m.; Nov 1 to Apr 30 6 a.m. to 8 p.m. Hikers only. Leashed dogs only; properly remove and dispose of dog waste.

Maps: USGS Fort McDowell topo map (trail not shown); McDowell Mountain Regional Park trail map; park website

Trail contacts: McDowell Mountain Regional Park; Maricopa County Parks and Recreation Office (see appendix)

Finding the trailhead: From I-10, exit east to Loop 202. Follow Loop 202 to AZ 87 (Beeline Highway). Go north on AZ 87 to Shea Boulevard. Go left on Shea Boulevard and drive to Fountain Hills Boulevard. Continue north until the road turns into McDowell Mountain Road. Continue north to McDowell Mountain Park Drive and turn left into the park. From the park entrance, drive 2.7 miles to a turn onto Thoms Thumb Drive and E. I. Rowland Campground. Turn left and drive 0.1 mile to a hiker parking area and the Wagner Trailhead on the road's right side (GPS: 33.694216, -111.730996).

The Hike

This 4.8-mile-long hike makes a wide circle around McDowell Mountain Regional Park. Following four trails—Wagner, Granite, Bluff, and Spur Trails—the hike offers great views, gentle grades, wildlife, and solitude. Bring plenty of water, especially if it's hot. Little shade is found along the trail.

Start at a parking lot and the Wagner Trailhead for the hike's first leg on the right side of Thoms Thumb Drive before it enters E. I. Rowland Campground. The signed trailhead has a shaded kiosk with park information and maps, and a picnic table shaded by a palo verde tree. Follow Wagner Trail north and then bend west with the campground to your left. After a mile, cross a closed service road that goes west to a maintenance building. Past the road is the junction of Wagner Trail and Granite Trail. Go right on Granite Trail for the next segment, which makes a horseshoe before ending at Bluff Trail. The left fork at the junction is Wagner Short Loop Trail (Hike 22).

Continue west skirting a wide wash. Near the McDowell Mountains, the trail dips across the wash and reaches a shallow canyon filled with granite boulders and mountain views. The wash offers fine bird-watching, with many species in the mesquite and palo verde trees.

At the boulders, Granite Trail bends southeast, passes an old stock tank, then follows the edge of a wash to a junction with Bluff Trail. Go left on Bluff Trail for the next segment, following a bluff above Stoneman Wash, a dry wash filled with gravel eroded from the McDowells. Continue to a junction with Stoneman Wash Trail on the floor of the wash. Continue on Bluff Trail and climb out of the wash to a junction with Granite Trail.

Go right on Granite Trail for a few hundred feet to a junction with Spur Trail. Keep left on Spur Trail and hike to the campground. End the trail opposite campsite 21 on Rock Nob Road. Go right on the road and follow it to Thoms Thumb Drive and then east to the trailhead and parking lot.

Miles and Directions

0.0 Start at the Wagner Trailhead on the right side of Thoms Thumb Drive west of McDowell Mountain Park Drive and the park visitor center. Hike north and then west on signed Wagner Trail north of the campground.

1.0 Reach a maintenance road. Cross and continue on the Wagner Trail.

1.1 Reach the junction of Wagner Trail and Granite Trail (GPS: 33.698623, -111.743364). Go right and hike northwest on Granite Trail.

1.6 Pass the junction of Granite Trail and Lariat Trail on the right. Keep left on Granite Trail.

1.7 Pass the junction of Granite Trail and Delsie Trail on the right. Go left on Granite Trail and descend into a wash and pass the junction of Granite Trail and Stoneman Wash Trail (GPS: 33.702579, -111.751511).

2.5 Reach granite boulders on the hillsides west of Granite Trail. Continue straight on the trail and bend southeast.

2.9 Reach the junction of Granite Trail and Bluff Trail (GPS: 33.696386, -111.757496). Go left and hike southeast on Bluff Trail.

3.7 Reach the junction of Bluff Trail and Stoneman Wash Trail in a wide wash (GPS: 33.695555, -111.744631). Continue straight and climb out of the wash.

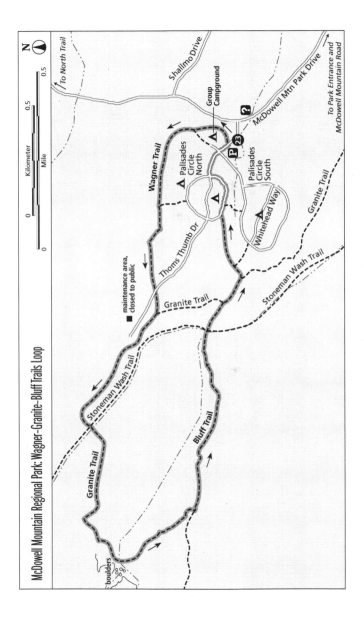

McDowell Mountain Regional Park: Wagner-Granite-Bluff Trails Loop

3.9 Meet the junction of Bluff Trail and Granite Trail (GPS: 33.694522, -111.742595). Go right and hike southeast on Granite Trail.

4.0 Reach the junction of Granite Trail and Spur Trail. Go left on Spur Trail and hike northeast toward the campground.

4.3 Reach Rock Nob Road opposite campsite #21 in the campground's north loop. Go right and walk on the road.

4.5 Reach the junction of Rock Nob Road and Thoms Thumb Drive. Go right on Thoms Thumb Drive and hike east.

4.8 Arrive back at the trailhead (GPS: 33.694216, -111.730996).

24 McDowell Mountain Regional Park: Lousley Hill Trail

An easy desert hike with cactus gardens and scenic views of the McDowell Mountains, Verde River valley, and the Four Peaks.

Distance: 1.2 miles
Hiking time: About 1 hour
Type of hike: Lollipop
Trail name: Lousley Hill Trail
Difficulty: Easy. Elevation gain is 285 feet.
Best season: Nov through Apr
Water availability: Water available at the campground trailhead
Restrictions: Park hours from May 1 to Oct 31 5 a.m. to 9 p.m.; Nov 1 to Apr 30 6 a.m. to 8 p.m. Hikers only; no mountain bikes or horses. Leashed dogs only; properly remove and dispose of dog waste.
Maps: USGS Fort McDowell (trail not shown); McDowell Mountain Regional Park trail map; park website
Trail contacts: McDowell Mountain Regional Park; Maricopa County Parks and Recreation Office (see appendix)

Finding the trailhead: From I-10, exit east onto Route 202 (Red Mountain Freeway). Follow Route 202 east to exit 13 (labeled "Country Club Drive" and "Payson") to AZ 87 (Beeline Highway). Drive north on AZ 87 for 11.9 miles to Shea Boulevard. Turn left onto Shea Boulevard and drive 2.8 miles to Fountain Hills Boulevard. Drive north on it for 4 miles and a sharp right bend where the road turns into McDowell Mountain Road. Continue north for 3.6 miles to McDowell Mountain Park Drive and turn left into the park. Follow the road through the park for 4.9 miles to Lousley Drive South. Turn right into Ironwood Picnic Area and drive 0.4 mile to the trailhead and parking lot on the right (GPS: 33.709655, -111.702288). The Lousley Hill

Trailhead (GPS: 33.709571, -111.701863) is on the south side of the road east of the parking area.

The Hike

This short hike winds to the top of 2,044-foot Lousley Hill, the high point of a range of hills in the northeast corner of McDowell Mountain Regional Park. The 1.2-mile lollipop trail offers superb views across the Verde River valley and plenty of cactus, including saguaro and teddy bear cholla, along the hike.

Start at the Lousley Hill Trailhead and walk south to a sandy wash below Lousley Hill. Bend left and hike the wash to a junction and take the left fork. Walk east down the wash and then leave the wash and climb into a shallow canyon. The stony trail threads up the canyon's left side to a ridge. Underfoot are rounded boulders and cobbles composed of basalt, a volcanic rock formed from lava, shaped by the ancestral Verde River, and deposited on gravel terraces.

Hike up the ridge (steepest part of the hike) to a rest bench shaded by a palo verde tree. A spectacular vista unfolds to the east with the blue ribbon of the Verde River meandering south. Beyond looms the distinctive, 7,657-foot Four Peaks and the Mazatzal Mountains.

Turn west and climb an easy grade along a broad ridge to the rounded summit of Lousley Hill. The hill's south slopes are dotted with sun-loving saguaros and dense mats of teddy bear cholla cacti. Don't brush against the cholla. The joints, lying on the ground or on the cacti's arms, will "jump" onto you. A pair of pliers is handy for removing them from bare skin.

From the hilltop, enjoy a 360-degree view and then hike to switchbacks that swing down the north slopes to the wash.

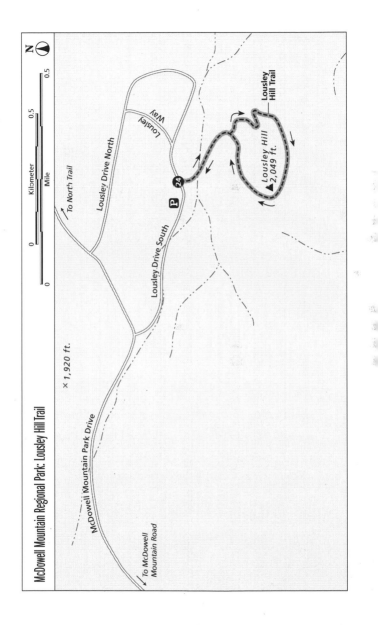

McDowell Mountain Regional Park: Lousley Hill Trail

At the wash, go left up the wash to the trail junction. Go left to the trailhead.

Miles and Directions

0.0 Start from the Lousley Hill Trailhead east of the parking lot on the south side of Lousley Drive.

0.2 Meet a trail junction in a wash and the start of a lollipop loop (GPS: 33.708333, -111.701417). Go left. Right fork is the return trail.

0.5 Stop at a bench atop the escarpment.

0.75 Reach the top of Lousley Hill (GPS: 33.705531, -111.701601).

1.0 Reach the first trail junction in the wash and go left.

1.2 Arrive back at the trailhead (GPS: 33.709571, -111.701863).

25 McDowell Mountain Regional Park: North Trail

This scenic loop hike treks across the remote desert landscape east of the rugged McDowell Mountains in the northern sector of McDowell Mountain Regional Park.

Distance: 2.9 miles
Hiking time: About 2 hours
Type of hike: Lollipop
Trail name: North Trail
Difficulty: Moderate. Elevation gain is 138 feet.
Best season: Nov through Apr
Water availability: Water available at the campground trailhead
Restrictions: Park hours from May 1 to Oct 31 5 a.m. to 9 p.m.; Nov 1 to Apr 30 6 a.m. to 8 p.m. Hikers and mountain bikers only; no horses. Leashed dogs only; properly remove and dispose of dog waste.
Maps: USGS Fort McDowell (trail not shown); McDowell Mountain Regional Park trail map; park website
Trail contacts: McDowell Mountain Regional Park; Maricopa County Parks and Recreation Office (see appendix)

Finding the trailhead: From I-10, exit east onto Route 202 (Red Mountain Freeway). Follow Route 202 east to exit 13 (labeled "Country Club Drive" and "Payson") to AZ 87 (Beeline Highway). Drive north on AZ 87 for 11.9 miles to Shea Boulevard. Turn left onto Shea Boulevard and drive 2.8 miles to Fountain Hills Boulevard. Drive north on it for 4 miles and a sharp right bend where the road turns into McDowell Mountain Road. Continue north for 3.6 miles to McDowell Mountain Park Drive and turn left into the park. Follow the park road for 5.4 miles from the park entrance station to Asher View Drive. Turn left and follow Asher View Drive for 0.5 mile to a parking lot on the right. The signed North Trailhead is on the opposite (west) side of the road (GPS: 33.719184, -111.696418).

The Hike

The North Trail is an excellent hike through an unspoiled Sonoran Desert ecosystem. The trail quickly leaves all traces of civilization behind, allowing hikers to experience the sights and sounds of the desert in solitude.

The hike starts on Asher View Drive, opposite the parking area. Hike west from the trailhead past to a Y-junction and turn right to begin the loop section. The trail heads northwest across washes and then bends west. Look for the 45-foot-high saguaro, a magnificent desert giant, alongside the trail. The Asher Hills, a couple of rocky knobs, flank the trail on its north side.

At a junction with Chuparosa Trail, keep left on North Trail. Tall saguaros scatter across the desert, among palo verde trees, buckhorn cholla cacti, clumps of hedgehog barrel cacti, and creosote bushes. Watch for some common mammals, including the blacktailed jackrabbit, antelope and rock squirrels, coyote, and javelina. Over one hundred bird species have been sighted here, including many migrants. Common birds are cactus wrens, roadrunners, ravens, Gila woodpeckers, phainopeplas, northern cardinals, and curve-billed thrashers. Raptors soaring overhead include Harris's hawks, red-tailed hawks, and turkey vultures.

The trail rolls across many washes before bending sharply east. Look right to a rounded hillock and higher Lousley Hill (Hike 24). The trail descends eastward to the first junction. Go right and walk to the hike's end.

Miles and Directions

0.0 Begin at the North Trailhead on the west side of Asher View Drive and hike west.

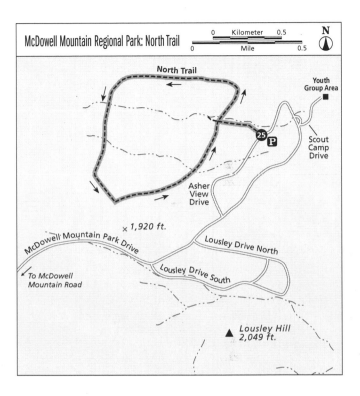

McDowell Mountain Regional Park: North Trail

North Trail

Youth Group Area

Scout Camp Drive

Asher View Drive

× 1,920 ft.

McDowell Mountain Park Drive

To McDowell Mountain Road

Lousley Drive North

Lousley Drive South

▲ Lousley Hill 2,049 ft.

0.1 Reach a junction and the start of the lollipop loop (GPS: 33.719017, -111.697705). Go right and hike northwest and then west on the trail.

1.6 Reach a junction with Chuparosa Trail (GPS: 33.715451, -111.713935). Keep left on North Trail and hike east and then northeast, dipping across many washes.

2.8 Return to the first junction and go right or east on the trail.

2.9 Arrive back at the trailhead (GPS: 33.719184, -111.696418).

26 Cave Creek Regional Park: Go John Trail

This superb loop hike threads through scenic desert canyons north of Phoenix.

Distance: 5.8 miles
Hiking time: 3–4 hours
Type of hike: Loop
Trail name: Go John Trail
Difficulty: Moderate. Cumulative elevation gain is 924 feet.
Best season: Nov through Apr
Water availability: Water available at the trailhead
Restrictions: Park hours from May 1 to Oct 31 5 a.m. to 9 p.m.; Nov 1 to Apr 30 6 a.m. to 8 p.m. Entry fee is charged. Leashed dogs only; properly remove and dispose of dog waste. Trail is multiuse; yield to horses. Follow Leave No Trace principles.
Maps: USGS Cave Creek; Maricopa County Cave Creek Regional Park map; park website
Trail contacts: Cave Creek Regional Park; Maricopa County Parks and Recreation Office (see appendix)

Finding the trailhead: From I-17 north of Phoenix, take exit 223 and drive east on Carefree Highway for 7.1 miles to North 32nd Street. Turn left on North 32nd Street and drive 1.6 miles north to Cave Creek Regional Park's entrance station. Pay entrance fee and follow Cave Creek Parkway northeast for 1 mile, passing a nature center, group picnic areas, and horse staging area, to a left turn on Mountain Road. Follow it north for 0.2 mile and turn left into a parking lot at the signed Go John Trailhead (GPS: 33.832809, -112.001149).

The park is also reached from AZ 101, the beltway around Phoenix. Exit AZ 101 on Scottsdale Road. Follow Scottsdale Road north to Carefree Highway. Turn left and follow Carefree Highway to North 32nd Street and the park entrance.

The Hike

Cave Creek Regional Park, spreading across desert foothills north of Phoenix, is a superb 2,922-acre Maricopa County parkland with over 11 miles of backcountry trails for hikers, mountain bikers, and horseback riders. The park offers wild and untamed country, despite lying just north of the Phoenix metropolis.

One of the park's best hikes is Go John Trail, a long but relatively easy loop hike that circles around 3,060-foot Cave Creek Peak. Other good hikes at the park include 1.9-mile Overton Trail, which edges along the west boundary before joining Go John Trail, and the out-and-back Clay Mine Trail. Check the park map for hike details.

Start at the signed Go John Trailhead at the north end of a parking lot at the end of Mountain Road off Cave Creek Parkway. The trail heads north up a sandy wash and then climbs to a low saddle. Descend along the west flank of Cave Creek Peak to a junction with Overton Trail. Continue north up a valley to a junction with Maricopa Trail on the park's northern boundary. Maricopa Trail heads north for 4.3 miles to Spur Cross Ranch Conservation Area, a Maricopa County parkland.

From here, the trail bends east and contours across cacti-strewn slopes to another major junction. Keep right on Go John and climb south to a saddle. Descend a broad wash, bend around a ridge, and climb a valley, passing saguaro cacti and palo verde trees. After good winter rains, look for wildflower carpets in March and April that color the dry landscape. After passing a junction with Quartz Trail, arrive at a third saddle and descend easy slopes to the trailhead.

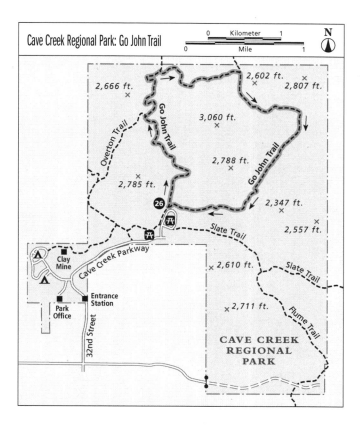

Cave Creek Regional Park: Go John Trail

2,666 ft. ×

2,602 ft. ×

× 2,807 ft.

3,060 ft. ×

Overton Trail

Go John Trail

2,788 ft. ×

2,785 ft. ×

Go John Trail

26

2,347 ft. ×

2,557 ft. ×

Slate Trail

Clay Mine

Cave Creek Parkway

× 2,610 ft.

Slate Trail

Entrance Station

Park Office

32nd Street

× 2,711 ft.

Flume Trail

CAVE CREEK REGIONAL PARK

Miles and Directions

0.0 Start at the Go John Trailhead (GPS: 33.832814, -112.001178).

1.3 Reach the junction with Overton Trail (GPS: 33.843658, -112.004645). Keep right on Go John Trail.

2.1 Reach a junction with Maricopa Trail at the park's north boundary (GPS: 33.849805, -112.002388). Go right on Go John Trail.

3.1 Reach a junction with a trail on the left (GPS: 33.848910, -111.990741). Keep right on Go John Trail and hike over Gunsight Pass, a low saddle.

4.5 Meet the junction with Quartz Trail on the left (GPS: 33.837445, -111.986261). Keep right and hike southwest on Go John Trail.

5.5 Reach a junction with Jasper Trail (GPS: 33.832283, -111.996766). Continue straight west on Go John Trail.

5.8 Arrive back at the alternate Go John Trailhead on the east side of the parking lot (GPS: 33.832644, -112.001029).

27 Spur Cross Ranch Conservation Area: Spur Cross and Metate Trails

Following two trails, this spectacular hike threads through untouched Sonoran Desert ecosystems filled with cactus gardens and mature saguaros, and follows Cave Creek, one of the few perennial streams in the Phoenix area.

Distance: 2.35 miles
Hiking time: 1–2 hours
Type of hike: Lollipop loop
Trail names: Spur Cross Trail, Metate Trail
Difficulty: Moderate. Cumulative elevation gain is 152 feet.
Best season: Nov through Apr
Water availability: None
Restrictions: Park hours from May 1 to Oct 31 5 a.m. to 9 p.m.; Nov 1 to Apr 30 6 a.m. to 8 p.m. Entry fee (cash only) is charged. Leashed dogs only; properly remove and dispose of dog waste. Part of the hike is multiuse; yield to horses. No bikes or horses allowed on Metate Trail. No camping or fires. Stay on designated trails. Follow Leave No Trace principles.
Maps: USGS New River Mesa; Maricopa County Spur Cross Ranch Conservation Area map; park website
Trail contacts: Spur Cross Ranch Conservation Area; Maricopa County Parks and Recreation Office (see appendix)

Finding the trailhead: From I-17 north of Phoenix, take exit 223 and drive east on Carefree Highway for 11.8 miles to North Cave Creek Road. Turn left on North Cave Creek Road and drive 3.4 miles north to Cave Creek and turn left on North Spur Cross Road. Drive north on Spur Cross Road for 4.2 miles to a large parking lot, picnic tables, and the informal trailhead near the conservation area's southern boundary (GPS: 33.886426, -111.951848).

The parkland is also reached from AZ 101, the beltway around Phoenix. From AZ 101, take exit 28 onto Cave Creek Road. Drive north on Cave Creek Road for 12.4 miles and turn left on North Spur Cross Road. Follow it north to the parking lot and trailhead.

The Hike

Spur Cross Ranch Conservation Area, lying 5 miles north of the town of Cave Creek, protects 2,154 acres of pristine Sonoran Desert on the historic Spur Cross Dude Ranch, which operated from 1928 to 1953. After ranch owner Warren Beaubien died in a plane crash on the ranch's airstrip, his wife Billie sold the property to investors. In 1996 they proposed a golf course, hotels, and luxury homes on the property, alarming environmentalists since the area boasts crucial habitat for native species, Hohokam ruins, and a lush riparian ecosystem along Cave Creek. The ranch was annexed by Cave Creek, which nixed the development. It was acquired by Maricopa County in 2001 and is now its crown jewel parkland.

Spur Cross Ranch offers flowing water, a rarity in this arid landscape, in Cave Creek, a 2-million-year-old stream that flows most of the year but brims with water from January through May. A dense mesquite woodland with stands of willows and scattered cottonwood trees lines its banks, while the floodplain along Metate Trail offers a spectacular collection of ancient saguaro cacti that tower above the creek. More saguaros blanket the arid mountainsides above the creek, making it one of the region's densest cactus gardens. The ranch also teems with wildlife, including javelina, coyote, and deer, over 120 bird species, as well as reptiles and amphibians. Almost ninety archaeological sites and petroglyph panels from the Hohokam occupation over a thousand years ago spread across the park.

The parkland offers 12.8 miles of hiking on eight trails that range from easy to strenuous. One of the best easy hikes follows wide Spur Cross Trail, an old ranch road, north from the trailhead to Cave Creek near the area's northern boundary, then follows scenic Metate Trail south alongside the creek, passing spectacular saguaros and threading through a thick mesquite bosque alive with birdsong and some of the twenty-seven dragonfly species in the park.

After hiking the trail, stop by adjoining 26-acre Jewel of the Desert Preserve, a Desert Foothills Land Trust property protecting about a mile of Cave Creek and its rich riparian ecosystem. Access its trail system from Spur Cross Ranch's parking lot by hiking Dragon Fly Trail along the creek or park at the preserve's roadside lot 0.2 mile south of the Spur Cross Trailhead.

Miles and Directions

0.0 Begin at an informal trailhead at the northwest corner of the parking lot. The parking lot at the site of the old Phoenix Mine is outside the conservation area boundary. Hike north on narrow Spur Cross Road.

0.10 Reach an entrance booth on the left (GPS: 33.887549, -111.951030) at the area's boundary. Pay the entrance fee (cash only) if it's open or at a self-pay station on the right side of the road. Go through a gate and continue north on the closed dirt road.

0.15 Reach a forked junction and the official Spur Cross Trailhead (GPS: 33.888470, -111.950756). A kiosk with info signs and a map is at the junction. Keep right on Spur Cross Trail (also called Maricopa Trail) and walk past restrooms. Continue north on the closed ranch road.

0.30 Reach a junction on the right with Fairy Duster Trail, an 0.6-mile loop (GPS: 33.890178, -111.950811). Hike north on Spur Cross Trail and descend a hill.

0.40 Reach the bottom of a wide wash, carved by Cottonwood Creek. Climb a hill on the north side and continue hiking north on the narrow road across a terrace dotted with saguaros.

0.95 Reach a junction on the right with signed Mariposa Hill Trail (GPS: 33.897635, -111.944958). Continue straight on Spur Cross Trail and begin descending north toward Cave Creek. Extra credit: Go right on Mariposa Hill Trail and hike 0.2 mile to the hill's summit, benches, and marvelous views of Cave Creek and the conservation area. Return to Spur Cross Trail for a 0.4-mile out-and-back side trip.

1.10 Reach a signed junction with Metate Trail on the left (GPS: 33.899720, -111.944890). Step left, go through a gate in a metal fence, and hike south on singletrack Metate Trail. No mountain bikes or horses are allowed on this trail. Hike along the edge of a bench above Cave Creek, passing saguaros and other cacti. Descend the trail to the floodplain along the creek.

1.30 On the floodplain (GPS: 33.898400, -111.948062), hike southwest through dense palo verde and mesquite trees and pass beneath mature saguaro cacti that tower above the trail. This is one of the best hike sections of any Phoenix trail.

1.50 Leave the saguaros and cross Cave Creek on a plank bridge to its west bank (GPS: 33.896595, -111.949973). Continue southwest across the floodplain on the creek's west side.

1.60 Past a shady bench, reach a junction on the left with Towhee Trail (GPS: 33.895593, -111.950341). Continue straight on Metate Trail and hike through a mesquite woodland. Extra credit: Go left on 0.2-mile Towhee Trail, which offers great views of Cave Creek before rejoining Metate Trail to the south.

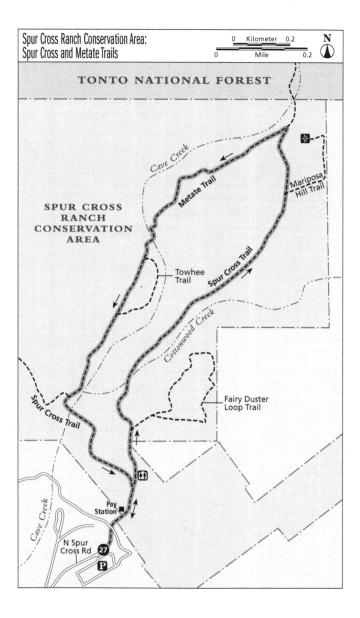

Spur Cross Ranch Conservation Area:
Spur Cross and Metate Trails

0   Kilometer   0.2
0   Mile   0.2

N

TONTO NATIONAL FOREST

Cave Creek

Metate Trail

SPUR CROSS
RANCH
CONSERVATION
AREA

Mariposa
Hill Trail

Towhee
Trail

Spur Cross Trail

Cottonwood Creek

Spur Cross Trail

Fairy Duster
Loop Trail

Cave Creek

Pay
Station

N Spur
Cross Rd   27

P

1.70 Reach the south junction with Towhee Trail. Continue south on Metate Trail.

1.75 Arrive at the Solar Oasis on the left (GPS: 33.893217, -111.951754). This lush site was reforested with ironwood trees around an old ranch well that pumps water with solar energy. The well is home to three endemic fish species, leopard frogs, and riparian plants. The rock-lined, shady pond makes a fine stop for a snack and sip of water. Do not wade in the pond. Continue south on Metate Trail, climbing onto dry slopes.

1.90 Reach a junction with Spur Cross Trail, an old ranch road here, and go left (GPS: 33.891207, -111.953256). Following signs reading "To Parking Lot," descend a hill past a shady bench and cross Cave Creek on a plank bridge. Climb a stony hill and pass a gate.

2.20 Return to the trailhead and the first junction where Spur Cross Trail forks. Go right and follow closed Spur Cross Road south past the entrance station.

2.35 Arrive back at the unofficial trailhead and parking lot (GPS: 33.886426, -111.951848).

28 Lost Dutchman State Park: Treasure Loop Trail

This scenic loop hike crosses rocky slopes below rugged cliffs and gullies below the towering western front of the legendary Superstition Mountains.

Distance: 2.4 miles
Hiking time: 1-2 hours
Type of hike: Loop
Trail name: Treasure Loop Trail (#56)
Difficulty: Moderate. Elevation gain is 515 feet.
Best season: Nov through Apr
Water availability: Water and restrooms at Cholla and Saguaro Day-Use Areas

Restrictions: Fee area. The park is open year-round. Main park gate and trails are open 6 a.m. to 8 p.m. Leashed dogs only; properly remove and dispose of dog waste.
Maps: USGS Goldfield; park map
Trail contacts: Lost Dutchman State Park; Tonto National Forest (see appendix)

Finding the trailhead: Drive east from Phoenix and I-10 on US 60/Superstition Freeway. Take exit 196 onto Idaho Road/AZ 88. Drive north on Idaho Road into Apache Junction and cross Old West Highway after 2 miles. Continue north on Idaho Road and after 1.7 miles, turn right on diagonal Apache Trail/AZ 88. Drive northeast on Apache Trail/AZ 88 for 4.9 miles and turn right into Lost Dutchman State Park. Follow the park road past the entrance station and at 0.3 mile go left and follow the road for 0.2 mile to Cholla Day-Use Area and parking lot for Treasure Loop. The Treasure Loop Trailhead is on the north side of the parking lot (GPS: 33.461178, -111.477505). Additional parking is in a lot opposite the day-use area's circular parking lot. The return loop of the trail can also be accessed at a trailhead and parking lot at Saguaro Day-Use Area. Park address: 6109 N Apache Trail, Apache Junction.

The Hike

The 320-acre Lost Dutchman State Park, at the western edge of the Superstition Mountains west of Phoenix, is named for the renowned Lost Dutchman Mine. The mine's myth began in 1892 when Jacob Walz, an old German prospector dying of pneumonia, revealed cryptic directions to a hidden gold mine on his deathbed. Walz said, "There's a great stone face looking up at my mine. If you pass three red hills you've gone too far. The rays of the setting sun shine on my gold. Climb above the mine and you can see Weavers Needle."

Using these vague directions, thousands of treasure seekers have tirelessly searched the Superstition Mountains for the fabulous lost lode. The treasure remains lost and geologists say gold isn't found in the range's volcanic rock. But old legends die hard, so the search for Walz's wealth continues.

The 2.4-mile Treasure Loop Trail offers a different kind of mother lode for day hikers—gorgeous scenery, distant views, unusual plants, and bracing desert air. The adventure begins at the Treasure Loop Trailhead on the north side of Cholla Day-Use Area in the state park.

Walk northeast to a gate along a fence that marks the boundary between the state park and Tonto National Forest. The trail ascends a broad outwash plain west of the Superstition Mountains, passing saguaro cacti. Saguaros, the symbol of Arizona, grow as tall as 50 feet, live 200 years, and weigh over 10 tons. Blooming in May and June, their white blossoms are Arizona's state flower. Other plants on the hike include palo verde trees, bursage, jojoba, and a variety of cactus species.

After passing Jacob's Crosscut Trail, the trail steepens and climbs around a blocky rock formation. Soaring 600-foot cliffs loom above the trail. The cliffs are formed by rocks deposited during periods of fiery volcanism between 15 and 24 million years ago. Most of the cliffs are composed of volcanic ash with harder basalt intrusions that were deposited as molten lava. Several prominent pinnacles rear left of the main cliff including the obvious Praying Hands, with a popular climbing route up a ridge.

At the halfway point, the trail reaches its 2,617-foot-high point below cliffs. A bench lets the weary rest their feet and enjoy scenic views. The mountain-studded horizon includes the White Tank Mountains, Camelback Mountain and Piestewa Peak above Phoenix, and the Usery and Goldfield Mountains.

The trail drops across a wash to Green Boulder, a large block colored by green lichen. Farther down is another bench near the junction of Treasure Loop Trail and Prospector's View Trail, a 0.7-mile path that rambles along the mountain base to Siphon Draw Trail.

Treasure Loop Trail switchbacks down a steep slope to another rest bench and Jacob's Crosscut Trail. Past the bench the hike levels and enters a "forest" of saguaro and chain cholla cacti. Finish by leaving the national forest at a gate and hiking through Lost Dutchman State Park to the parking lot's east side.

Miles and Directions

0.0 Start from the Treasure Loop Trailhead right of the restrooms at Cholla Day-Use Area (GPS: 33.461262, -111.477647). Hike northeast on the wide trail.

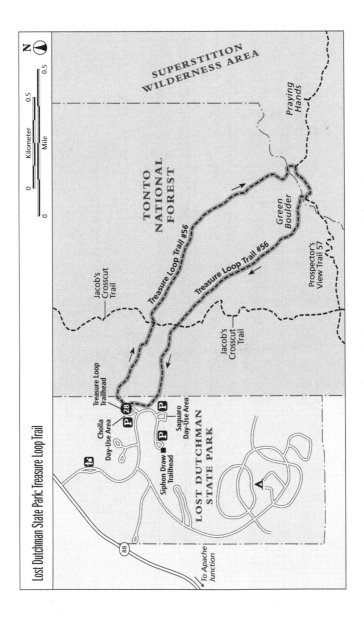

Lost Dutchman State Park: Treasure Loop Trail

0.1 Reach the Tonto National Forest boundary and pass through a gate in a barbed wire fence. Follow the easy trail east across a bajada studded with cacti, ocotillo, and palo verde trees.

0.4 Reach the junction with Jacob's Crosscut Trail (GPS: 33.459769, -111.472476). Continue straight on signed Treasure Loop Trail toward the mountains.

1.2 Arrive at the trail's high point below the Superstition escarpment (GPS: 33.452071, -111.464795). Descend across steep slopes.

1.3 Reach a junction with Prospector's View Trail (#57) at a saddle upslope from Green Boulder, a blocky rocky formation (GPS: 33.452386, -111.465266). Keep right and hike past the south side of Green Boulder on Treasure Loop Trail. Continue west on the trail on gentle slopes.

1.9 Reach a junction with Jacob's Crosscut Trail (GPS: 33.458689, -111.472726). Continue straight on the trail signed "Saguaro Parking Lot."

2.2 Reach a Y-junction (GPS: 33.459382, -111.475485). Keep right to return to Cholla Day-Use Area and the trailhead. The left trail goes to Saguaro Day-Use Area.

2.3 Reach another junction and keep right to return to Cholla Day-Use Area (GPS: 33.459758, -111.477027). Hike north near the road to the Cholla parking lot (social trails cut left to the lot). The left trail at the junction jogs over to Saguaro Day-Use Area.

2.4 Arrive back at the trailhead (GPS: 33.461178, -111.477505).

29 Lost Dutchman State Park: Siphon Draw Trail

This excellent scenic hike gently ascends slopes into a steep-walled canyon sliced into the west flank of the Superstition Mountains.

Distance: 3.8 miles
Hiking time: 2–3 hours
Type of hike: Out and back
Trail name: Siphon Draw Trail (#53)
Difficulty: Moderate. Elevation gain is 1,070 feet.
Best season: Nov through Apr
Water availability: Water available at the Siphon Draw Trailhead and Saguaro and Cholla Day-Use Areas

Restrictions: Fee area. The park is open year-round. Main Park gate and trails are open 6 a.m. to 8 p.m. Leashed dogs only; properly remove and dispose of dog waste.
Maps: USGS Goldfield; park map
Trail contacts: Lost Dutchman State Park; Tonto National Forest (see appendix)

Finding the trailhead: Drive east from Phoenix and I-10 on US 60/Superstition Freeway. Take exit 196 onto Idaho Road/AZ 88. Drive north on Idaho Road into Apache Junction and cross Old West Highway after 2 miles. Continue north on Idaho Road and after 1.7 miles, turn right on diagonal Apache Trail/AZ 88. Drive northeast on Apache Trail/AZ 88 for 4.9 miles and turn right into Lost Dutchman State Park. Follow the park road past the entrance station and at 0.3 mile go left and follow the road past Cholla and Saguaro Day-Use Areas for 0.4 mile to a parking lot for the Siphon Draw Trailhead (GPS: 33.459356, -111.480003) at the road's end. Park address: 6109 N Apache Trail, Apache Junction.

The Hike

The Superstition Mountains, protected by 159,757-acre Superstition Wilderness Area, is a rugged mountain range east of Phoenix. The range, the alleged site of the famed Lost Dutchman Mine, is creased by deep canyons and lorded over by desert peaks and cliffs. Towering rock ramparts form the range's western edge, making a formidable scenic backdrop to Lost Dutchman State Park. The 320-acre park, with a 134-site campground and picnic areas, offers a network of superb trails on the sloping bajada below the escarpment.

One of the best is 1.9-mile Siphon Draw Trail, an excellent hike that climbs from the Siphon Draw Trailhead to a sharp canyon sliced into towering cliffs. The hike yields excellent views and a riotous carpet of wildflowers during the spring months.

Get underway at the Siphon Draw Trailhead and hike south on Siphon Draw Trail (the first section is Discover Trail (DI). When the trail reaches the campground, jog left and follow the trail along the campground's eastern edge to a junction. Turn left here on Siphon Draw Trail and hike southeast on an old mine road through saguaro cacti and other desert plants including bursage, palo verde trees, jojoba bushes, prickly pear cacti, chain cholla, and ocotillos.

East of the campground, the trail passes through a gate on the boundary between the state park and national forest. Continue past a junction with Jacob's Crosscut Trail on the stony trail toward the cliffs. Brittlebushes blanket slopes along the path, coloring them in spring with brilliant yellow flowers. Below the cliffs, meet an old road that runs north past a building's foundation to the abandoned site of the Palmer Mine, named for its owner, Dr. Ralph Palmer. The mine, staked in 1886, yielded copper and gold ores in a 265-foot-deep shaft. After the mine closed in 1950, it was a well until it was covered over.

Past the mine, the trail narrows to singletrack, and continues climbing toward the mouth of Siphon Draw. North of the trail loom 600-foot-high cliffs formed of volcanic rock. Suction Gully is the precipitous canyon sliced into the ramparts above the trail. Across the canyon to the south are more cliffs, broken into buttresses, minarets, castles, and ridges. The rock fin with an overhanging west face that sits on the slope below the main cliff is imaginatively called Crying Dinosaur. A clever eye can sort out the resemblance from a distance. Look for the head, neck, mouth, and a vertical crack that looks like a tear.

The trail dips across a wash and steadily ascends steeper slopes into the narrow canyon. The trail scrambles to the turn-around point in a box canyon floored with worn boulders. A dry waterfall, which sometimes runs in springtime, sits at the east end of the box. Sit and rest here, enjoy scenic views, and sip water before heading back to the trailhead.

Adventurous hikers can continue up the canyon on an unmaintained trail that leads to the top of the 4,861-foot Flatiron, a huge wedge of rock that overlooks Siphon Draw. The trail heads up the dry streambed and then clambers uphill through boulders and thorny bushes to the Flatiron's summit.

Miles and Directions

0.0 Begin at the Siphon Draw Trailhead at the southwest corner of the parking lot (GPS: 33.453567, -111.479972). Hike south on the trail toward Lost Dutchman Campground.

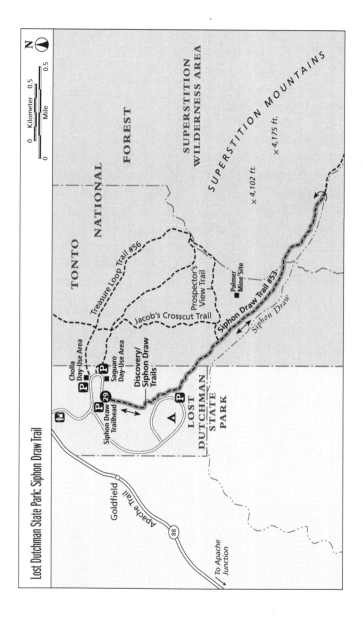

Lost Dutchman State Park: Siphon Draw Trail

N

0   Kilometer   0.5

0   Mile   0.5

TONTO NATIONAL FOREST

SUPERSTITION WILDERNESS AREA

SUPERSTITION MOUNTAINS

x 4,102 ft.

x 4,175 ft.

Treasure Loop Trail #56

Prospector's View Trail

Jacob's Crosscut Trail

Siphon Draw Trail #53

Palmer Mine Site

Siphon Draw

Cholla Day-Use Area

Saguaro Day-Use Area

Discovery/ Siphon Draw Trails

Siphon Draw Trailhead

29

LOST DUTCHMAN STATE PARK

Goldfield

Apache Trail

88

To Apache Junction

0.2 Reach a junction north of the campground and go left. Hike southwest and cross a wash.

0.35 Cross a paved road on the right side of the campground (GPS: 33.455050, -111.479536), with cabins on the left.

0.45 Reach a junction east of the campground and go left on Siphon Draw Trail (GPS: 33.453578, -111.479095). Hike southeast across open terrain. A right turn at the junction leads to an alternative trailhead in the campground.

0.6 Pass through a gate and barbed fence into Tonto National Forest (GPS: 33.452281, -111.476915). Continue southeast on the trail.

0.8 Reach a junction with Jacob's Crosscut Trail on the left (GPS: 33.450707, -111.474741). Continue straight.

1.2 Reach a junction with an old road to Palmer Mine (GPS: 33.446520, -111.470216). Keep straight on the main trail.

1.55 Enter a narrowing canyon and follow the rough trail below high cliffs on the north side of a wash.

1.9 Reach the hike's end point by a dry waterfall in Siphon Canyon (GPS: 33.441961, -111.460332). Turn around here and follow the trail back west.

3.8 Arrive back at the trailhead (GPS: 33.459356, -111.480003).

30 Peralta Regional Park: Saguaro Loop Trail

You want to see saguaros? Head to Peralta Regional Park east of Phoenix to admire magnificent stands of mature cactus along scenic Saguaro Loop Trail.

Distance: 1.8 miles
Hiking time: About 1 hour
Type of hike: Lollipop
Trail names: Stargazing Trail, Saguaro Loop Trail
Difficulty: Moderate. Elevation gain is 242 feet.
Best season: Oct through Apr
Water availability: No water available in the park; toilets near the trailhead
Restrictions: Fee area, day-use pass required (may be purchased online). Day-use hours from sunrise to 10 p.m. Main entry gates are locked at 10 p.m. and reopen at dawn. Closed on Christmas Day. Leashed dogs only; properly remove and dispose of dog waste. No glass, ceramic, or breakable plastic bottles. Stay on existing roads and trails. No shooting. The park is tobacco free, no smoking.
Maps: USGS Florence Junction; Peralta Regional Park website and park map
Trail contact: Peralta Regional Park (see appendix)

Finding the trailhead: Drive east from Phoenix on US 60/Superstition Freeway to Peralta Road just past milepost 204. Turn north on Peralta Road (FR 77) and drive 4.9 miles to a signed right turn into the park. Drive south on dirt on Entry Road past a fee station and take the first left turn. Drive east past a large parking lot with restrooms to the Main Trailhead and a parking lot on the left when the road bends right. The Main Trailhead is on the north side of the parking strip (GPS: 33.366942, -111.369605).

The Hike

Opened in January 2023, Peralta Regional Park, a 498-acre natural area administered by Pinal County, offers almost 10 miles of multiuse trails, picnic sites, a campground that includes seven backpacking sites, and plenty of solitude and scenery. The park borders Peralta Road, which heads north from the park entrance to popular Peralta Trail (Hike 31).

One of the park's best hikes follows Stargazing Trail past a site for telescopes to watch the night sky to Saguaro Loop Trail, which threads past a cactus garden filled mature saguaros and other species including teddy bear cholla and prickly pear cacti. The primitive trail is easy to follow with well-marked junctions and spectacular scenery, including views of the Superstition Mountains to the north.

Beginning at the Main Trailhead, the hike drops into a wash to Stargazing Node, a circular sitting area with wide sky views, then climbs to a junction with Saguaro Loop Trail. This lovely path makes a loop through an open valley and traverses below rugged volcanic cliffs rimming desert peaks.

If you still have a hiking itch after doing the hike, check out the park's other trails, including 1.1-mile Oro Vista Loop, 2.6-mile Desperado Trail, and 0.3-mile North Star Trail which ends at a high point with roomy views. The 0.5-mile accessible Interpretive Trail is an easy loop with a hardened surface for wheelchairs and strollers, six educational panels, and plenty of benches.

Miles and Directions

0.0 Start at the Main Trailhead and hike into a wash filled with saguaros.

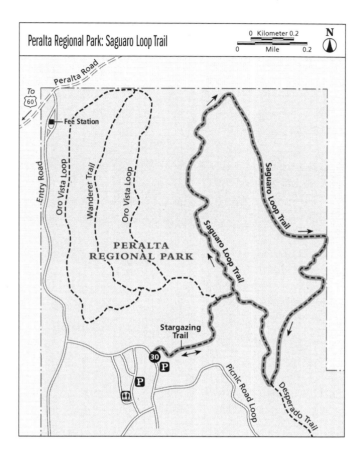

Peralta Regional Park: Saguaro Loop Trail

0.05 Climb onto a bench and reach Stargazing Node, a plaza for setting up a telescope and observing the night sky. Continue east and then north along the edge of a wash.

0.2 Cross an old ranch road and reach a junction (GPS: 33.368583, -111.367267) and the start of Saguaro Loop. Go left to start the loop. The trail on the right is the return path. Hike north across rolling terrain covered with prickly pear and cholla cacti and towering saguaros. The trail steadily gains elevation.

0.7 Reach the north end of the loop and superb views north of the rugged Superstition Mountains and mature saguaros (GPS: 33.373661, -111.367382). Follow the trail south, contouring across a steep hillside below high cliffs on Point 2,753.

0.9 Descend into a cactus-filled valley between peaks, skirt a barbed wire fence on the park's eastern boundary, and drop into a wide wash.

1.1 Climb out of the wash (GPS: 33.369297, -111.364910) and follow the trail up brushy slopes below cliffs rimming Point 2,546 and then south past Hole in the Rock in a trailside outcrop into a valley.

1.4 Reach the south end of the loop and a junction with Desperado Trail (GPS: 33.366204, -111.366151). Go right past an old mine and descend into the broad valley.

1.6 Reach the junction at the start of Saguaro Loop and turn left toward Stargazer Trail. Hike west along a wash and pass Stargazing Node.

1.8 Arrive back at the trailhead (GPS: 33.366942, -111.369605).

31 Superstition Wilderness Area: Peralta Trail

This excellent scenic hike climbs up Peralta Trail to Fremont Pass and views into the heart of Superstition Wilderness Area east of Phoenix.

Distance: 4.5 miles (round-trip)
Hiking time: 3–4 hours
Type of hike: Out and back
Trail name: Peralta Trail (#102)
Difficulty: Moderately challenging. Elevation gain is 1,340 feet.
Best season: Nov through Apr
Water availability: None
Restrictions: No mountain bikes or mechanized vehicles. Group size is limited to 15 people. Horses not recommended on trail. Follow Leave No Trace principles.
Maps: USGS Weavers Needle; Superstition Wilderness Area map; Tonto National Forest map
Trail contact: Tonto National Forest (see appendix)

Finding the trailhead: Drive east from Phoenix on US 60/Superstition Freeway to Peralta Road just past milepost 204. Turn north on Peralta Road (FR 77) and drive 7.2 miles to a parking lot at the road's end (GPS: 33.397411, -111.347989) and the trailhead. Parking is available at the trailhead and at a lot 0.2 mile south of the trailhead. Do not park along the road. Car break-ins occur at the parking lots. Stow all valuables out of sight or carry with you. The Peralta Trailhead is at road's end on the north side of the parking area.

The Hike

The 2.25-mile Peralta Trail is one of Arizona's most popular and busiest backcountry trails. The trail strikes north up a spectacular canyon lined with cliffs, spires, and hoodoos and ends on lofty Fremont Saddle with a stunning view north of soaring Weavers Needle and the surrounding Superstition Mountains.

The wide trail is easy to follow with mostly gentle grades. Pit toilets are at the trailhead but no drinking water. Bring plenty of water and sports drinks for your hike, especially on hot days. Other excellent hikes begin from the Peralta Trailhead, including Bluff Springs and Lost Dutchman Trails.

Begin at the Peralta Trailhead and hike north to an obvious trail junction. Keep left and enter Superstition Wilderness Area on Peralta Trail. A right turn leads to Bluff Springs and Lost Dutchman Trails. The trail heads north along a dry streambed into Peralta Canyon. A creek sometimes trickles after winter rains. Cross and recross the creek bed as the trail ascends northward. Shady rest spots hide beneath oaks and sumac along the trail—a welcome respite for cooling down.

Towering pinnacles and cliffs, composed of volcanic rock, line the canyon walls. Many rock layers are composed of tuff, a rock deposited as ash from erupting volcanoes. Desert varnish, a brown patina of iron oxides, covers the rock surface and obscures its natural pale color. Higher up the canyon, the trail crosses sections of bare bedrock. After steadily climbing, the trail reaches 3,766-foot Fremont Saddle, the hike's turnaround point.

The view from the saddle is one of the best in central Arizona. The landmark Weavers Needle, a 4,553-foot volcanic neck, punctures the northern skyline. The rugged peak, named for 19th-century mountain man, trapper, explorer, and prospector Pauline Weaver (1797–1867), figures prominently in the Lost Dutchman Mine legend. Linger at the saddle, munch a power lunch, and enjoy marvelous views.

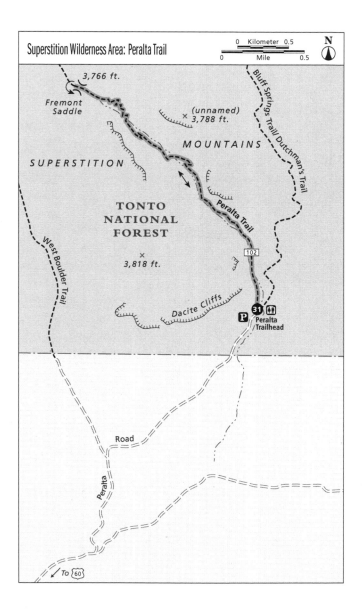

Superstition Wilderness Area: Peralta Trail

0   Kilometer   0.5

0   Mile   0.5

N

3,766 ft.

Fremont
Saddle

× (unnamed)
3,788 ft.

Bluff Springs Trail/Dutchman's Trail

MOUNTAINS

SUPERSTITION

Peralta Trail

TONTO
NATIONAL
FOREST

× 3,818 ft.

West Boulder Trail

102

Dacite Cliffs

P

31

Peralta
Trailhead

Road

Peralta

To 60

After resting, retrace your steps down the trail. Experienced hikers can return via rugged 2.7-mile Cave Trail (#233), which follows the ridgeline east of Peralta Canyon. The trail is hard to follow in places but offers more stellar views.

Miles and Directions

0.0   Start from the Peralta Trailhead at the north side of the parking lot. Hike north on Peralta Trail up Peralta Canyon.

0.01 Reach a junction with Dutchman Trail (#104). Keep left on Peralta Trail.

2.25 Reach Fremont Saddle (GPS: 33.415727, -111.364794). Turn around here and retrace the trail back south.

4.5   Arrive back at the trailhead (GPS: 33.397606, -111.347874).

32 White Tank Mountain Regional Park: Black Rock Long Loop Trail

This scenic hike loops across low hills and a cacti–studded outwash plain along the eastern edge of the White Tank Mountains.

Distance: 1.35 miles

Hiking time: About 1 hour

Type of hike: Loop

Trail name: Black Rock Long Loop Trail

Difficulty: Moderate. Elevation gain is 96 feet.

Best season: Nov through Apr

Water availability: Water available at the trailhead and picnic area

Restrictions: Park hours from May 1 to Oct 31 5 a.m. to 9 p.m.; Nov 1 to Apr 30 6 a.m. to 8 p.m. Hikers only; no mountain bikes or horses. Leashed dogs only; properly remove and dispose of dog waste. Dogs are not allowed on trails if temperatures exceed 100°F; violators are punished by fines and possible jail time. Glass bottles prohibited.

Maps: USGS White Tank Mountains SE (trail not shown); White Tank Mountain Regional Park trail map; park website

Trail contact: Maricopa County Parks and Recreation Office (see appendix)

Finding the trailhead: Drive west from Phoenix on I-10 to Cotton Lane (exit 124). Exit here and drive north on Cotton Lane for 7 miles to Olive Avenue. Turn left (west) and drive 5 miles to the park entrance. Enter the park on White Tank Mountain Road, pass the entrance booth, and drive 1.4 miles to a short road on the right signed "Black Rock Loop Trailhead" and "Area #4." Turn right and park in a large lot. The Black Rock Loop Trailhead is on the west side of the parking lot (GPS: 33.583516, -112.501453). Park address: 20304 W. White Tank Mountain Rd., Waddell.

The Hike

The eastern flank of the White Tank Mountains, a rugged range forming Phoenix's western skyline, is protected in Maricopa County's 29,271-acre White Tank Mountain Regional Park. Several deep canyons, including Ford, Willow, Mesquite, and Waterfall Canyons, slice into the range. The White Tank Mountains were named for the many natural water tanks, or tinajas, found in the narrow canyons, chiseled out of white granite by tumbling boulders after torrential thunderstorms. These natural catchments provide water for thirsty animals and birds during dry spells.

The Black Rock Long Loop Trail is a fun and easy loop hike across the sloping outwash plain below the mouth of Waterfall Canyon. The mostly level trail introduces unique desert plants, as well as offers spectacular views of the mountains and outdoor galleries of Hohokam rock art. The first part of the hike is part of 0.5-mile Black Rock Short Loop, a shorter accessible hike. Interpretive signs along this trail enhance your understanding of the Sonoran Desert.

The hike starts at Area 4 with shaded picnic tables, restrooms, and water. From the trailhead, walk west and cross the road to a Y-junction. Take the right fork. The first barrier-free trail section is wide and flat. The trail runs past a low hill and across an apron of gravel washed from Waterfall Canyon to the west.

Many cactus species flourish on this well-drained surface. Look for buckhorn cholla, tall saguaros, and teddy bear cholla. This cactus, its joints covered with sharp spines, appears soft and cuddly from a distance. Up close, it's a different matter. The spines hook and grab hikers who are minding their own

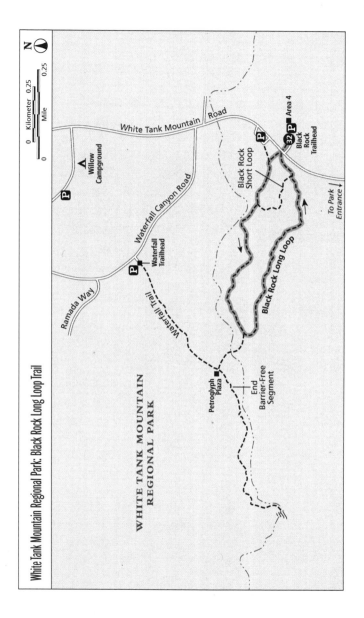

White Tank Mountain Regional Park: Black Rock Long Loop Trail

N

0   Kilometer   0.25

0   Mile   0.25

Willow Campground

Ramada Way

Waterfall Canyon Road

White Tank Mountain Road

P

Waterfall Trailhead

P

Waterfall Trail

WHITE TANK MOUNTAIN REGIONAL PARK

Petroglyph Plaza

End Barrier-Free Segment

Black Rock Short Loop

P

Black Rock Long Loop

32 P Area 4

Black Rock Trailhead

To Park Entrance

business. Smart hikers carry pliers to extricate cactus spines from shoes and skin.

Past a hill, the trail passes a junction where Black Rock Short Loop Trail goes left and returns to the trailhead. The hike continues straight across the bajada and edges above a deep wash. At the hike's halfway point is another junction. A short spur trail goes right to Petroglyph Plaza on Waterfall Trail. The main trail swings left here and heads southeast below a ridge studded with dark boulders and stately saguaros on a steep slope. Look for petroglyph panels scattered across boulders above the trail's right side. Continue east to the road and trailhead.

Miles and Directions

0.0   Start at the Black Rock Trailhead on the west side of the parking. Walk west and cross White Tank Mountain Road.

0.05 Reach a junction on the west side of the road (GPS: 33.583861, -112.502069). Take the right fork (also part of Black Rock Short Loop). The left fork is the return trail. Hike northwest and after 200 feet pass a junction with a spur trail that comes from an alternative parking lot to the right.

0.2   Look for petroglyphs on the rocky hill to the left.

0.22 Reach the junction of Black Rock short and long loops on the west side of the hill (GPS: 33.584798, -112.504611). Keep right on Black Rock Long Loop Trail and hike west.

0.7   Reach a junction with a spur trail that goes right for 0.1 mile to Waterfall Trail (GPS: 33.585333, -112.510942). Keep left on the main trail and hike southeast.

1.1   Look for petroglyphs on the trail's right side.

1.2   Reach the south junction of Black Rock Long Loop and Short Loop Trails (GPS: 33.583428, -112.503219). Go right on the wide trail.

1.3 Return to the first trail junction and the start of the loop at the road. Cross road and walk east toward the parking lot.

1.35 Arrive back at the trailhead (GPS: 33.583516, -112.501453).

33 White Tank Mountain Regional Park: Waterfall Trail

Follow this easy, accessible trail across open slopes to petroglyph-covered boulders, a rocky canyon, and a dry waterfall.

Distance: 1.8 miles
Hiking time: About 1 hour
Type of hike: Out and back
Trail name: Waterfall Trail
Difficulty: Easy. The first 0.5-mile section is barrier free and wheelchair accessible. Elevation gain is 245 feet.
Best season: Nov through Apr
Water availability: Water and restrooms at the trailhead
Restrictions: Park hours from May 1 to Oct 31 5 a.m. to 9 p.m.; Nov 1 to Apr 30 6 a.m. to 8 p.m. Hikers only; no mountain bikes or horses. Leashed dogs only; properly remove and dispose of dog waste. Glass bottles prohibited.
Maps: USGS White Tank Mountains SE topo (trail not shown); White Tank Mountain Regional Park trail map; park website
Trail contact: Maricopa County Parks and Recreation Office (see appendix)

Finding the trailhead: Drive west from Phoenix on I-10 to Cotton Lane (exit 124). Exit here and drive north on Cotton Lane for 7 miles to Olive Avenue. Turn left (west) and drive 5 miles to the park entrance. Drive into the park on White Tank Mountain Road, pass the entrance booth, and drive 2.1 miles and turn left on Waterfall Canyon Road. Drive 0.4 mile and turn left into a parking lot and the Waterfall Trailhead (GPS: 33.589643, -112.507639). Park address: 20304 W. White Tank Mountain Rd., Waddell.

The Hike

Waterfall Trail is a pleasant 1.8-mile round-trip hike with gentle grades to a dry waterfall in the heart of Waterfall Canyon. This trek is an excellent adventure in the late afternoon when cool shade floods the canyon. The first 0.5 mile of the trail is barrier free, with a hardened surface for easy access and plenty of rest benches.

Begin at the Waterfall Trailhead and head southwest on a wide, level path up the broad mouth of Waterfall Canyon. Cobbles and boulders washed out of the mountains by flash floods form this sloping outwash plain. Desert trees, including mesquite, ironwood, and palo verde, scatter across the stony ground. Steep mountain slopes to the right are dotted with saguaro cacti, along with teddy bear cholla, buckhorn cholla, and hedgehog barrel cacti.

Petroglyph Plaza near the trail's midpoint offers a fenced area with a bench beside boulders darkened with a surface patina of manganese and iron oxides. Petroglyphs blanket the dark surface of the boulders. The Hohokam people, who hunted game and gathered edible plants here over 1,000 years ago scratched geometric designs into the rock surface. Look up the hill to the right for more petroglyphs.

The accessible, barrier-free section of trail ends another 0.1 mile past Petroglyph Plaza beside a deep wash. This is the turn-around point for wheelchairs. Past here the canyon pinches down, and immense rock walls loom above the trail. The White Tank Mountains, a fault block range, are composed of granite and metamorphic gneiss deposited as long ago as a billion years.

More rock art is above an old steel stock tank put here years ago to water thirsty cattle. Petroglyphs cover boulders above the trail. Keep your eyes open to see this Native American art show. The rock art site is closed to visitation. Admire from the trail and continue west up the boulder-choked canyon lined with towering rock walls.

The last trail section clambers past large boulders to the waterfall at the hike's end. To reach water tanks below the waterfall, scramble up polished granite to the base of the dry waterfall. Two large tanks, usually filled with water, sit below the falls. The waterfall only runs after heavy rain, usually from severe storms in the summer monsoon. Don't drink or bathe in the murky water—it's vitally important to local animals and birds, especially in dry periods. The cliffs surrounding the waterfall are treacherous. Avoid climbing on water-polished rock. It's deceptively dangerous, and fatalities have occurred here.

Miles and Directions

0.0 Start at the Waterfall Trailhead on the south side of the parking lot. Hike southwest on the wide trail.

0.4 Reach fenced Petroglyph Plaza on the right (GPS: 33.586651, -112.512617). Look for Hohokam petroglyphs on boulders above the trail to the right. Just past the plaza is the junction with a 0.1-mile spur trail that goes southeast to Black Rock Long Loop Trail. Continue straight on the main trail.

0.5 Reach the end of the barrier-free trail beside a wash (GPS: 33.585608, -112.514093). Rest on a couple benches and read an interpretive sign. Turn around here or continue southwest on the rougher trail.

0.8 Reach an old stock tank on the right (GPS: 33.585289, -112.518856). Look for petroglyphs on boulders above the trail. The area beyond the viewpoint is closed to hikers.

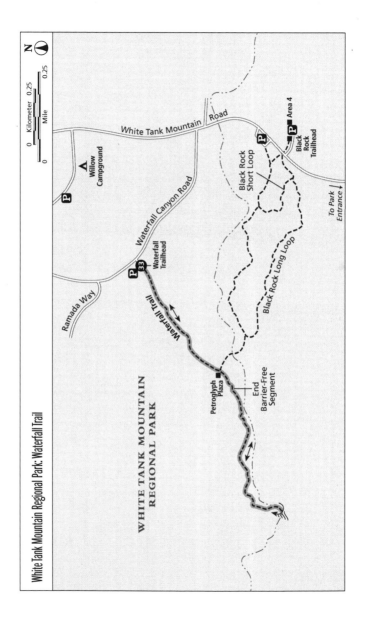

White Tank Mountain Regional Park: Waterfall Trail

Continue on the trail, threading through boulder piles and climbing steps in the narrowing canyon.

0.9 Reach the base of the dry waterfall in a cul-de-sac canyon surrounded by towering cliffs (GPS: 33.583895, -112.519461). After enjoying this magical spot, return northeast on the trail.

1.8 Arrive back at the trailhead (GPS: 33.589643, -112.507639).

34 Estrella Mountain Regional Park: Gila Trail and Baseline Trail Loop

A pleasant hike across open desert terrain with easy grades and scenic views below the Sierra Estrella mountains southeast of Phoenix.

Distance: 2.3 miles, including accessible Gila Trail loop
Hiking time: About 1 hour
Type of hike: Lollipop loop
Trail names: Gila Trail (GL), Baseline Trail (BA)
Difficulty: Easy. Elevation gain is 290 feet.
Best season: Nov through Apr
Water availability: Water available at the trailhead and picnic area
Restrictions: Park hours from May 1 to Oct 31 5 a.m. to 9 p.m.; Nov 1 to Apr 30 6 a.m. to 8 p.m. Hikers only on Gila Trail. Baseline trail is multiuse. Leashed dogs only; properly remove and dispose of dog waste. Glass bottles prohibited. No smoking; no alcoholic beverages. Yield to horses on the trail.
Maps: USGS Perryville, Tolleson, Avondale SE, and Avondale SW (trail not shown); Maricopa County Park map; park website
Trail contact: Maricopa County Parks and Recreation Office (see appendix)

Finding the trailhead: From Phoenix and Scottsdale, drive west on I-10 to Estrella Parkway exit or exit 126. From the exit, drive south for 7 miles and turn left on Vineyard Road. Follow this road for 2.5 miles to the entrance to Estrella Mountain Regional Park. From the entrance station, follow Casey Abbott Parkway to a junction; go left on Casey Abbott Drive North (paralleling 143rd Drive on the left) to the Baseline Trailhead and parking area on the right (GPS: 33.381926, -112.370167).

The Hike

Estrella Mountain Regional Park encompasses 19,840 acres of arid desert and rugged mountains on the southwest edge of the Valley of the Sun. The pristine park, which became the first regional park in the Maricopa County Park system in 1954, offers 43 miles of trails for hiking, mountain biking, and horseback riding.

One of the best trails is 2.1-mile Baseline Trail in the northwest corner of the park. The easily accessed trail forms a loop hike around a low foothill that rises above the flat valley to the north. The first and last hike sections follow barrier-free, wheelchair-accessible Gila Trail.

Start at the signed "Gila/Baseline Trailhead" on the southeast side of a large parking lot. Follow accessible Gila Trail, passing a few benches, to a fork where Gila Trail forms a loop. Go left on the trail. The right trail is the return path. Hike south to another junction at a ramada. Go left on the Baseline Spur Trail and hike to a third junction. Baseline Trail forms a loop from this point. Go left at the junction; the right trail is the return hike.

The trail heads up a ravine to a saddle, then contours right across the sunny slopes of a knobby hill, passing several trail junctions. Keep right and stay on the main path. Enjoy fine views south into the heart of the Sierra Estrella (Star Mountains in English), along with the usual assortment of lower Sonoran Desert plants including creosote, staghorn cholla cactus, barrel cactus, slender saguaro cactus, and palo verde and ironwood trees.

The trail bends north and passes a junction with Baseline Trail Spur which goes left to an alternative trailhead. Continue north through washes and return to the junction at the

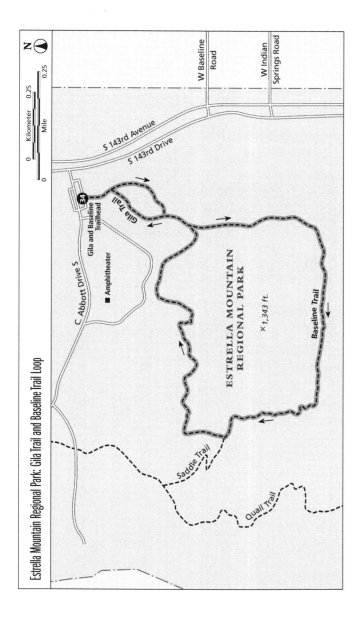

Estrella Mountain Regional Park: Gila Trail and Baseline Trail Loop

start of the Baseline Trail loop. Go left and hike west to the junction of the Baseline and Gila Trails. Keep left on Gila Trail and hike west to the trailhead.

Miles and Directions

0.0 Start at the trailhead for Gila and Baseline Trails. Hike south on wide, accessible Gila Trail.

0.1 Reach the first Gila Trail junction (GPS: 33.380775, -112.369949). Keep left and continue south.

0.2 Reach the second Gila Trail junction at a ramada (GPS: 33.379017, -112.370994). Go left on Baseline Spur Trail. The right trail is the return segment.

0.3 Reach a Y-junction at the start of the Baseline Trail loop (GPS: 33.377808, -112.371511). Go left to start the loop. The right trail is the return.

0.7 Reach a junction with a spur trail on the left (GPS: 33.373563, -112.373468). Keep straight on Baseline Trail and hike west.

0.9 Reach a junction with a spur trail (GPS: 33.373829, -112.377014). Stay straight on Baseline Trail. The left fork goes 0.1 mile to Rainbow Trail.

1.3 Reach a junction on the left with Saddle Trail (GPS: 33.376978, -112.379881). Keep right on Baseline.

1.5 Meet a junction with a spur trail to left (GPS: 33.378385, -112.378468). Keep straight and hike east on the main trail.

2.0 Reach the junction at the beginning of the Baseline Trail loop. Go left or north on Baseline Trail and gently descend north.

2.1 Reach the junction of Baseline Trail and Gila Trail. Take the left branch of Gila Trail and hike west.

2.3 Arrive back at the trailhead (GPS: 33.381725, -112.370271).

35 Hassayampa River Preserve: Palm Lake and Mesquite Meander Loop

This loop hike explores lush bird habitats and riparian woodlands along the placid Hassayampa River in the desert oasis of Hassayampa River Preserve northwest of Phoenix.

Distance: 1.13 miles
Hiking time: About 1 hour
Type of hike: Loop
Trail names: Palm Lake Loop (barrier free), Brill Bypass, Mesquite Meander, Willow Walkway
Difficulty: Moderate. Elevation gain is 32 feet.
Best season: Oct through Apr
Water availability: Water available at visitor center
Restrictions: Fee area. Free for children under 12. Park House from May 1 to Oct 31, Wed to Sun, 7 a.m. to 4 p.m.; trails close at 3:30 p.m.; Nov 1 to Apr 30, Wed to Sun, 8 a.m. to 5 p.m.; trails close at 4:30 p.m.

No pets allowed in the preserve. Stay on existing trails. Do not collect plants, rocks, or anything else in the park. No fires or cookstoves, smoking, or wading or swimming—no water access. Do not feed wildlife. Endangered and threatened bird species nest at the park; do not play audio recordings of these species, approach nests, or harass birds. No trash cans—pack it in and pack it out.
Maps: USGS Wickenburg; park website and map
Trail contact: Hassayampa River Preserve (see appendix)

Finding the trailhead: From downtown Phoenix and I-15, drive northwest on US 60 to the junction of US 60 and AZ 74. Continue 6.3 miles and turn left across the divided highway to Hassayampa River Preserve. Go through a gate and drive southwest on a dirt road for 0.2 mile to a parking lot on the right and the visitor center and trailhead on the left (GPS: 33.932588, -112.694600). Pay an entry fee in the visitor center then walk through to the trailhead on its east side. Visitor center address: 49614 US 60, Wickenburg.

The Hike

The 113-mile-long Hassayampa River, beginning near Prescott, flows south to the Gila River. While most of the river flows subsurface, it perennially flows in Hassayampa River Canyon Wilderness and Hassayampa River Preserve northwest of Phoenix. The 770-acre preserve, jointly managed by the Maricopa County Parks and Recreation Office and The Nature Conservancy, protects lush vegetation along the sluggish river and crucial habitat for rare plants and almost 300 species of birds.

The preserve offers over 5 miles of hiking on seven trails that thread through a cottonwood and willow forest and a mesquite bosque on the river's floodplain, and encircle Palm Lake, a desert oasis lined with towering California fan palms and providing waterfowl habitat.

The described hike, following Palm Lake Loop, a barrier-free trail, and Mesquite Meander trails, explores the best of Hassayampa Nature Preserve and allows opportunities for nature study, bird-watching, and the sound of murmuring water, a desert rarity. The park is open for only a few days a week and hours are limited, so plan before visiting. Besides excellent bird-watching, the preserve offers picnicking and ranger-led nature walks.

Before taking the hike, stop inside the visitor center to learn about the area's natural history, including crucial habitats—desert upland, riparian forest, and desert aquatic ecosystems, and some of the 4,000 species that live here. The center also details the human history including the native Yavapai people who lived here until the 1850s, and settlers like Frederick Brill who had a farm, orchard, and fish farm in the 19th century and its later incarnations as a dude ranch and trailer park before The Nature Conservancy bought 333 acres along the Hassayampa River for preservation.

Miles and Directions

0.0 Start at the trailhead by the rear door of the visitor center. Walk down a ramp, go left on a wide trail, and walk east.

0.04 Reach a five-way junction with park information and rules posted on a metal grid (GPS: 33.932482, -112.694268). Go straight on Palm Lake Loop Trail. The return trail is on the left. Mesquite Meander Trail angles right and Lion's Trail and River Ramble are sharply right. Walk past picnic tables below tall palm trees and continue east on the mesquite-shaded trail on the south side of Palm Lake, passing info signs about birds and benches.

0.22 Reach a junction at the southeast corner of Palm Lake (GPS: 33.931776, -112.691329) and go right on Brill Bypass. The return loop is straight ahead. Walk southeast on Brill Bypass.

0.27 Reach a junction with Mesquite Meander (GPS: 33.931325, -112.691592). Go left on it and hike south 75 feet to another junction and go left on Mesquite Meander. Hike east on the shady trail, passing a turnoff to a viewing point on the Hassayampa River. On the preserve's east side, the trail bends left (GPS: 33.929746, -112.689026) and goes west toward Palm Lake.

0.71 Reach a junction with Palm Lake Loop and an overlook with a bench on the lake's east side (GPS: 33.931937, -112.691349). Enjoy the view of the blue lake, fan palms, tall trees, and birdsong, then go right on Palm Lake Loop.

0.83 On the lake's north side, reach a junction with Willow Walkway on the left (GPS: 33.933241, -112.691720). Go left on the quiet path through thick woods.

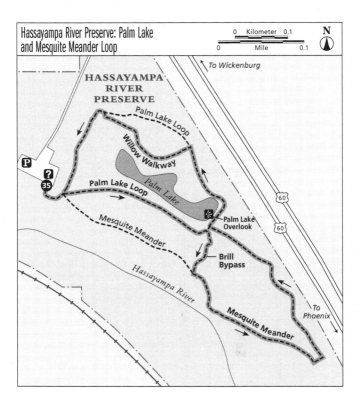

Hassayampa River Preserve: Palm Lake and Mesquite Meander Loop

0.97 Reach a junction with Palm Lake Loop (GPS: 33.933831, -112.693443) and go left. Following signs to "Visitor Center," follow the trail south past a magnificent stand to California fan palms.

1.09 Return to the five-way trailhead and go right to the visitor center.

1.13 Arrive back at the trailhead (GPS: 33.932588, -112.694600).

Appendix: Contact Information

Cave Creek Regional Park
37019 N. Lava Lane
Cave Creek, AZ 85331
(602) 505-2930 ext. 8
www.maricopacountyparks.net/park-locator/
cave-creek-regional-park/

Estrella Mountain Regional Park
14805 West Vineyard Avenue
Goodyear, AZ 85338
(602) 506-2930 ext. 6
www.maricopacountyparks.net/park-locator/
estrella-mountain-regional-park/

Glendale Parks and Recreation
5970 W. Brown Street
Glendale AZ 85302
(623) 930-2820
Park ranger: (623) 695-3004
www.glendaleaz.com/live/amenities/parks_facilities
_trails/regional_parks/thunderbird_conservation
_park

Hassayampa River Preserve
49614 US 60/89
Wickenburg, AZ 85390
(602) 506-2930 ext. 9
www.maricopacountyparks.net/park-locator/
hassayampa-river-preserve/

Lost Dutchman State Park
6109 N. Apache Trail
Apache Junction, AZ 85119
(480) 982-4485
https://azstateparks.com/lost-dutchman

Maricopa County Parks and Recreation Office
41835 N. Castle Hot Springs Road
Morristown, AZ 85342
(602) 506-2930
www.maricopacountyparks.net/

McDowell Mountain Regional Park
16300 McDowell Mountain Park Drive
Fountain Hills, AZ 85268
(602) 506-2930 ext. 3
www.maricopacountyparks.net/mcdowell
-mountain-regional-park/

McDowell Sonoran Conservancy
15300 N. 90th Street Suite 400
Scottsdale, AZ 85260
(480) 998-7971
www.mcdowellsonoran.org/

McDowell Sonoran Preserve
7447 E. Indian School Road, Suite 300
Scottsdale, AZ 85251
(480) 312-7013
www.scottsdaleaz.gov/preserve

North Mountain Visitor Center
12950 North 7th Street
Phoenix, AZ 85022
(602) 343-5125
www.northmountainvisitorcenter.org

Peralta Regional Park
Pinal County Parks
17975 E. Peralta Road
Gold Canyon, AZ 85118
(520) 509-3555
www.pinal.gov/1204/Peralta-Regional-Park

Phoenix Parks and Recreation Department
Phoenix City Hall
200 W. Washington Street
Phoenix, AZ 85003
(602) 262-3111
www.phoenix.gov/parks

Pinnacle Peak Park
26802 N. 102nd Way
Scottsdale, AZ 85262
(480) 312-0990
www.scottsdaleaz.gov/parks/pinnacle-peak-park

Scottsdale Parks and Recreation
3939 N. Drinkwater Boulevard
Scottsdale, AZ 85251
(480) 312-3111
www.scottsdaleaz.gov/parks

Spur Cross Ranch Conservation Area
44000 N. Spur Cross Road
Cave Creek, AZ 85331
(602) 506-2930 ext. 8
www.maricopacountyparks.net/park-locator/
spur-cross-ranch-conservation-area/

Tonto National Forest
2324 E. McDowell Road
Phoenix, AZ 85006
(602) 225-5200
www.fs.usda.gov/tonto

Tonto National Forest
Cave Creek Ranger District
40202 North Cave Creek Road
Scottsdale, AZ 85262
(480) 595-3300
www.fs.usda.gov/tonto

Tonto National Forest
Mesa Ranger District
5140 E. Ingram Street
Mesa, AZ 85205
(480) 610-3300
www.fs.usda.gov/tonto

Usery Mountain Regional Park
3939 N. Usery Pass Road
Mesa, AZ 85207
(602) 506-2930 ext. 4
www.maricopacountyparks.net/park-locator/
usery-mountain-regional-park/

White Tank Mountain Regional Park
20304 W. White Tank Mountain Road
Waddell, AZ 85355
(602) 506-2930 ext. 5
www.maricopacountyparks.net/park-locator/
white-tank-mountain-regional-park/

About the Author

Stewart M. Green, a veteran writer and photographer, has hiked, climbed, photographed, and traveled across the American West and the world in search of memorable images and experiences to document. Stewart, a freelance writer and photographer for Globe Pequot, FalconGuides, and Every Adventure Publishing, has written and photographed over sixty-five travel and outdoor adventure books. These include *Scenic Driving Arizona*; *Best Climbs Phoenix, Arizona*; *Rock Climbing Arizona*; *Scenic Driving California's Pacific Coast*; *Rock Art: The Meanings and Myths Behind Ancient Ruins in the Southwest and Beyond*; and *Hiking Waterfalls Utah*. His photographs and writing are published in many magazines, books, websites, and ads. He is currently writing a memoir of his early climbing days in Moab and Colorado and a historical novel about the Rocky Mountain gold rush.

THE TEN ESSENTIALS OF HIKING

American Hiking Society

Whether you plan to be gone for a couple of hours or several months, make sure to pack these items. Become familiar with these items and know how to use them.

Find other helpful resources at AmericanHiking.org/hiking-resources

1. Appropriate Footwear

2. Navigation

3. Water (and a way to purify it)

4. Food

5. Rain Gear & Dry-Fast Layers

6. Safety Items (light, fire, and a whistle)

7. First Aid Kit

8. Knife or Multi-Tool

9. Sun Protection

10. Shelter